Better Homes and Gardens®

WOOD

FAVORITE TOYS

YOU CAN MAKE

Dear Toymaker,

Congratulations on having just purchased another fine-quality product from the editors of *WOOD*® magazine. If you enjoy building toys for friends or loved ones, you're going to appreciate this book. In fact, the staff and I think it's the best toy-project book ever published. But that's for you to decide.

On the pages that follow, you'll find the 26 most popular toy projects ever featured in *WOOD*® magazine, complete with step-by-step instructions, easy-to-understand drawings, how-to photographs, cutting diagrams, a bill of materials, and finishing pointers. **We've built all of these projects ourselves in the *WOOD*® magazine shop** and have worked out all the construction bugs so that you will have a successful building experience the first time, every time.

Here's hoping that you have a great time making these projects. Get ready for lots of compliments on your craftsmanship—and probably some hugs from the lucky children who receive your heirloom gifts.

Larry Clayton

Larry Clayton, Editor
WOOD® magazine

Editor: Larry Clayton
Managing Editor: Marlen Kemmet
Designer: Perry McFarlin

Publisher: William R. Reed
Senior Vice President, Publishing Director: Adolph Auerbacher
Business Manager: Terry Unsworth

Cover Photograph: Hopkins Associates
©COPYRIGHT Meredith Corporation, 1991.
All Rights Reserved.
Printed in the U.S.A.

WOOD®

FAVORITE TOYS

YOU CAN MAKE

Tuff-Stuff Tow Truck 4

Delight a special youngster with this toddler-sized tow truck.

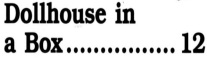

Board of Education 10

This bright learning toy teaches colors and shapes.

Dollhouse in a Box 12

When playtime ends, this two-story house collapses neatly into a carrying-case base.

Plow-Time Tractor 18

Step-by-step, we'll teach you how to make this toy, plus the wheels!

Red Baron Airplane............20

With your help, a youngster can build this high-flyin' project.

Rocking Horse ..24

Youngsters will wait in line to mount this trusty steed.

Long-Haul Auto Transport..28

Bandsaw this portable garage to shape in a matter of minutes.

"Big Apple" Bank.....30

A colorful way to encourage thrift.

Snow-Loving Open Sleigh 32

Designed in Minnesota for kids wherever there's snow.

Cherry Doll Cradle 38

Our adaptation of a traditional Scandinavian design.

Yo-Yo 44

Turn out a stack of these long-time favorite toys.

Zoo Carousel 45
The spinning action of this wild-animal carousel will catch their eye.

Fat Cat® Heavy Haulers .. 48
We've got ourselves a convoy here, good buddy!

Fat Cat® Bulldozer 53
To fill the needs of every little sandbox construction foreman.

Waddles the Duck 56
A pull toy with an irresistible waddle as it walks.

Doll Stroller 61
This stroller will definitely light up her eyes. Oh what a gift!

Playtime Express Train 64
All aboard for a project toddlers— and their parents—just can't resist.

Doll Furniture 70
A wonderful doll-sized swing, desk, and high chair.

Tip-Top Tops ... 75
Turn one of these nifty playthings in just minutes.

Baja Buggy 76
Rip-roaring racer stylized after a West Coast beach buggy.

Tiny Table and Chairs 78
Build this charming set from just one 4×8 sheet of plywood.

Four-Pack Car Caddy 83
A portable garage with four band-sawed playtime vehicles.

Rubber-Band Dragster 84
It pops a wheelie and races across the floor for fun.

Building-Block Castle 86
Versatile castle designed for your little prince or princess.

Tug-a-Lug Tugboat 90
For bathtub maneuvers, give this small-but-proud boat a try.

Barnstorming Biplane 92
Kids will love this toy reminiscent of the World War I Curtiss JN-4.

Index 96
For locating that special toy in a hurry, turn to this page.

No Job Too Small!

TUFF-STUFF TOW TRUCK

Need a lift? Then delight a special youngster with this toddler-sized tow truck. It maneuvers playroom byways with ease and takes lots of abuse, just like the big ones. (We know because 2½-year-old Justin road-tested ours right here in the WOOD Shop.) Best of all, each tow truck comes with a full, 5-year, 5,000-smile warranty.

Note: If your tow truck will be used outdoors, we recommend a slow-set epoxy adhesive. Otherwise, use woodworker's glue. Either way, be sure to epoxy the steering wheel to the steering dowel.

Building the chassis

1 Lay out and cut the chassis base (A) and boom support (B) to shape using the Parts View drawing of each as a guide. Cut the notch in B with a bandsaw or jigsaw. (Do *not* drill the ¾" holes in A or B yet.)

2 Rout a ⅜" round-over on the top and bottom edges of the tail end of the chassis where shown in the Chassis Assembly drawing, *below.* Glue and clamp B onto A, keeping the front ends flush.

3 To make the axle housings (C, D), rip a 30"-long piece of ¾" oak to 2". Then, crosscut the board in

half leaving two boards just under 15" long. Cut or rout a ½" groove ½" deep, centered down the length of one face of one of the boards. Now, cut one C and one D from each 15" board to the lengths listed in the Bill of Materials.

4 Glue and clamp the two C's together and the two D's together, with the grooves facing out and the edges flush.

5 Measure and mark the location of the rear-axle housing (C) on the bottom of the chassis base (A) where dimensioned in the Parts

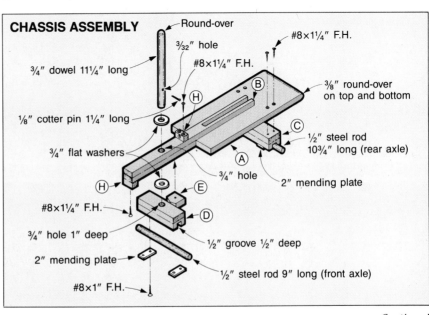

CHASSIS ASSEMBLY

- Round-over
- ³⁄₃₂" hole
- #8×1¼" F.H.
- ¾" dowel 11¼" long
- ⅜" round-over on top and bottom
- ⅛" cotter pin 1¼" long
- ¾" flat washers
- ½" steel rod 10¾" long (rear axle)
- 2" mending plate
- ¾" hole
- #8×1¼" F.H.
- ¾" hole 1" deep
- ½" groove ½" deep
- 2" mending plate
- ½" steel rod 9" long (front axle)
- #8×1" F.H.

Continued

TUFF-STUFF TOW TRUCK

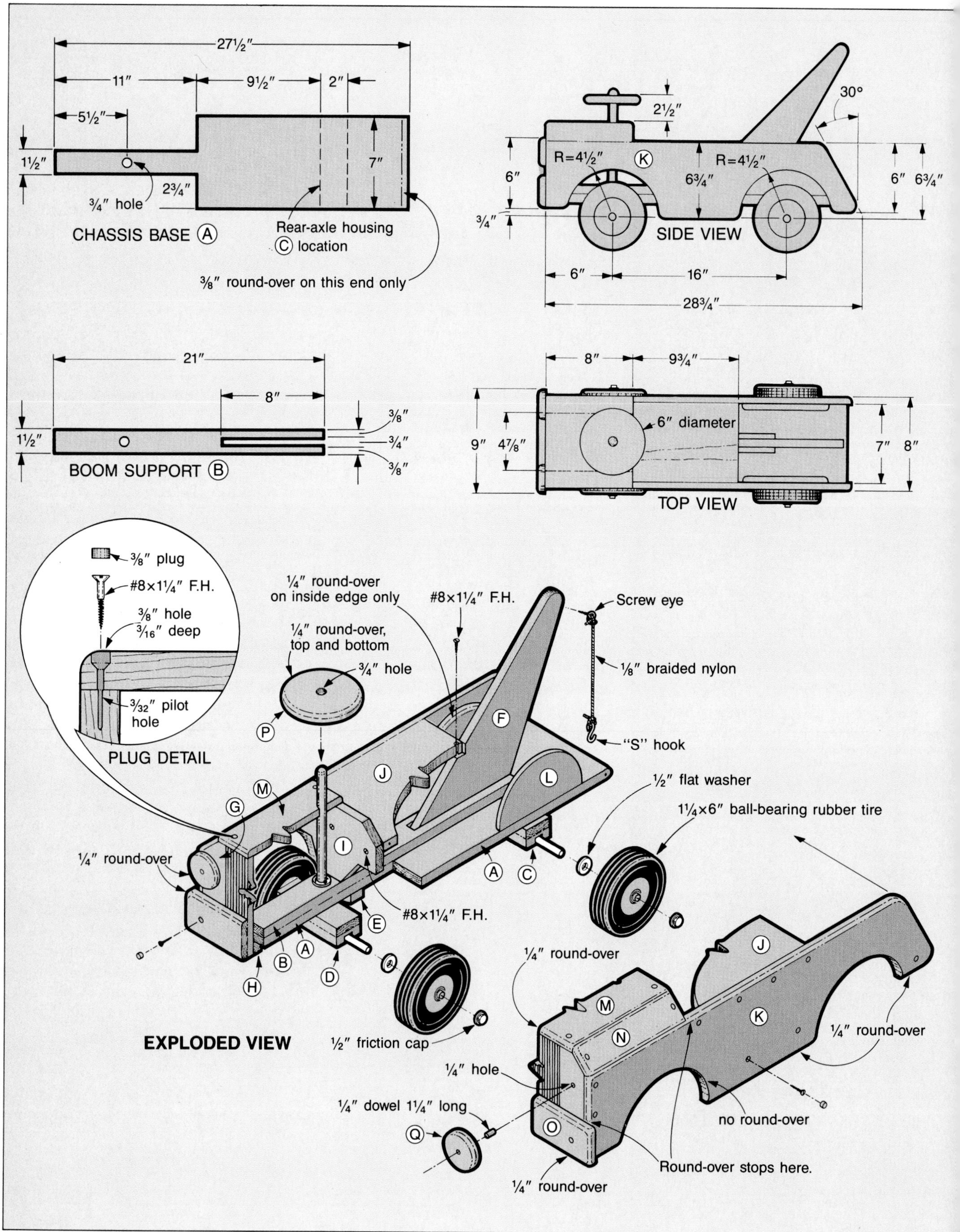

27 1/2"
11"
9 1/2"
2"
5 1/2"
1 1/2"
7"
2 3/4"
3/4" hole
CHASSIS BASE (A)
Rear-axle housing (C) location
3/8" round-over on this end only
30°
2 1/2"
R=4 1/2"
(K)
R=4 1/2"
6"
6 3/4"
6"
6 3/4"
3/4"
SIDE VIEW
6"
16"
28 3/4"
21"
8"
3/8"
3/4"
3/8"
1 1/2"
BOOM SUPPORT (B)
8"
9 3/4"
6" diameter
9"
4 7/8"
7"
8"
TOP VIEW
3/8" plug
#8×1 1/4" F.H.
3/8" hole 3/16" deep
3/32" pilot hole
PLUG DETAIL
1/4" round-over on inside edge only
#8×1 1/4" F.H.
Screw eye
1/4" round-over, top and bottom
3/4" hole
1/8" braided nylon
(P)
(F)
"S" hook
(J)
(L)
1/2" flat washer
(M)
(G)
1 1/4×6" ball-bearing rubber tire
(I)
1/4" round-over
(A)
(C)
#8×1 1/4" F.H.
(E)
(B)
(A)
(D)
(H)
1/4" round-over
(J)
(M)
(K)
(N)
1/4" round-over
EXPLODED VIEW
1/2" friction cap
1/4" hole
1/4" dowel 1 1/4" long
(Q)
(O)
no round-over
Round-over stops here.
1/4" round-over

Cutting Diagram

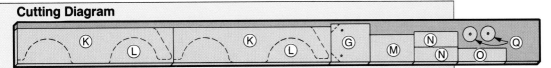

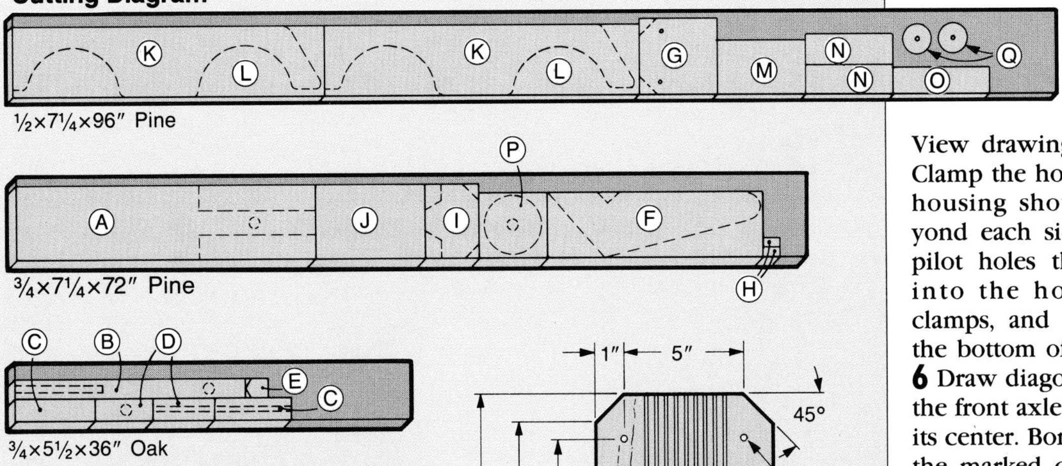
K
L
K
L
G
M
N
N
O
Q
½x7¼x96″ Pine
P
A
J
I
F
H
¾x7¼x72″ Pine
C
B
D
E
C
¾x5½x36″ Oak

Bill of Materials

Part	Finished Size* T	W	L	Material	Qty.
A	¾″	7″	27½″	pine	1
B	¾″	1½″	21″	oak	1
C*	1½″	2″	7¼″	oak (laminated)	1
D*	1½″	2″	5½″	oak (laminated)	1
E	¾″	1½″	2″	oak	1
F	¾″	5⅜″	20″	pine	1
G	½″	7″	7″	pine	1
H	¾″	¾″	1½″	pine	2
I	¾″	7″	4¾″	pine	1
J	¾″	7″	9¾″	pine	1
K	½″	6¾″	28¾″	pine	2
L	½″	4½″	9″	pine	2
M	½″	4⅞″	8″	pine	1
N	½″	2¼″	8″	pine	2
O	½″	2½″	9″	pine	1
P	¾″	6″ diam.		pine	1
Q	½″	2½″ diam.		pine	2

*Parts marked with a * are cut larger initially, then trimmed to finished size. Please read the instructions before cutting.

Supplies: #8x1″ flathead wood screws, #8x1¼″ flathead wood screws, #8x2″ flathead wood screws, ¾″ dowel stock (oak or birch), 2—¾″ flat washers, 4—2″ mending plates with predrilled holes and screws (Stanley catalog no. CD995-R—2″), ⅛″ cotter pin 1¼″ long, 4—½″ flat washers, 4—½″ friction caps, 4—1¼x6″ ball-bearing rubber tires, ½x20″ steel rod (for axles), ⅛″ braided nylon (for tow rope), 1″ S hook, 1—small (#10) screw eye, paraffin, wood putty, sanding sealer, oil-based exterior enamel paint—flat black and gloss yellow

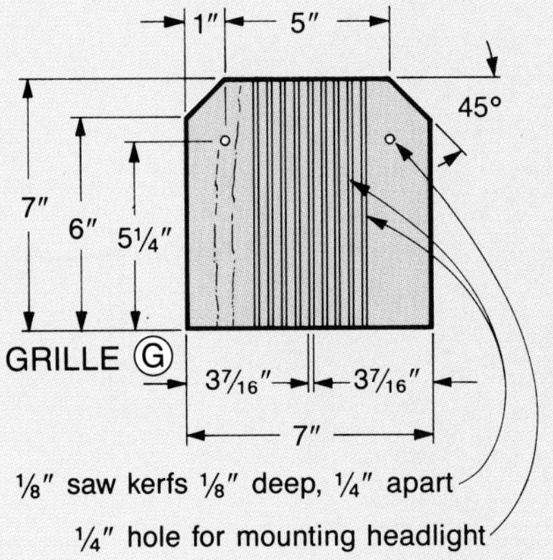
1″
5″
45°
7″
6″
5¼″
GRILLE G
3⁷⁄₁₆″
3⁷⁄₁₆″
7″
⅛″ saw kerfs ⅛″ deep, ¼″ apart
¼″ hole for mounting headlight

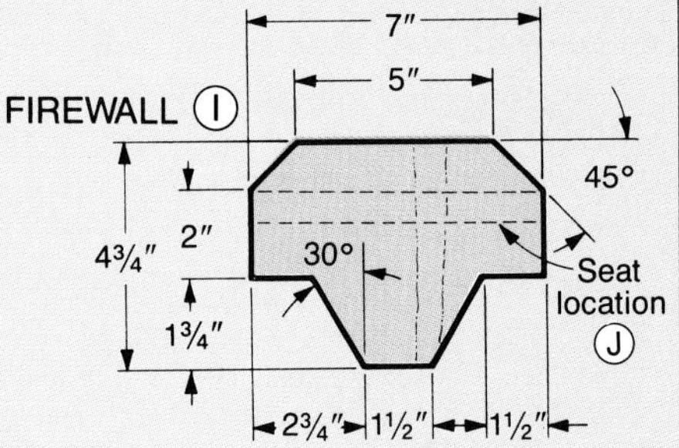
7″
5″
FIREWALL I
45°
4¾″
2″
30°
Seat location J
1¾″
2¾″
1½″
1½″

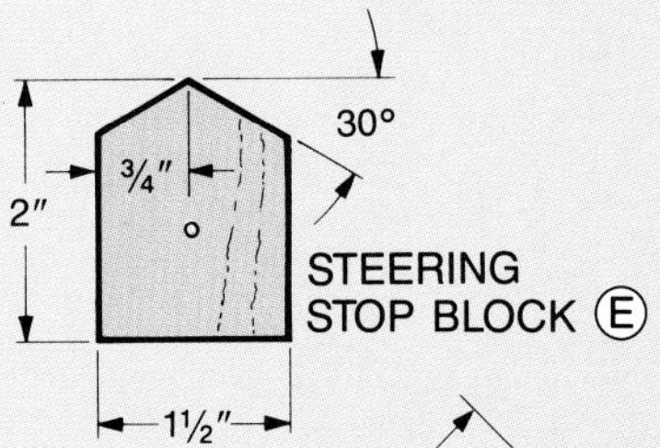
30°
2″
¾″
STEERING STOP BLOCK E
1½″

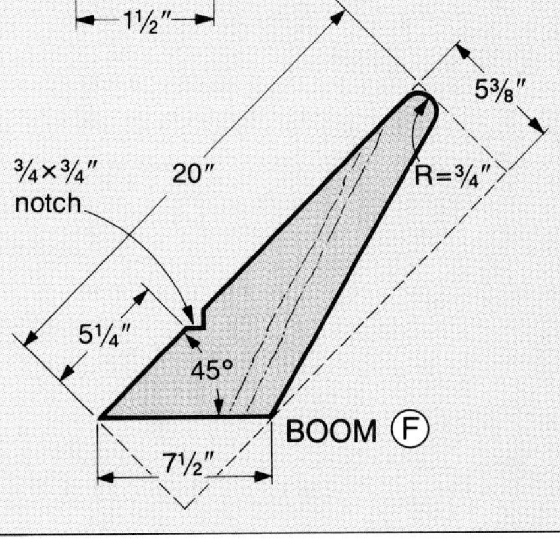
5⅜″
¾x¾″ notch
20″
R=¾″
5¼″
45°
BOOM F
7½″

View drawing of A, *opposite page.* Clamp the housing to the base (the housing should protrude ⅛″ beyond each side of the base). Drill pilot holes through the base and into the housing, remove the clamps, and glue and screw C to the bottom of A.

6 Draw diagonal lines on the top of the front axle housing (D) to locate its center. Bore a ¾″ hole 1″ deep at the marked centerpoint in the top of D for the steering dowel. Using the Parts View drawings of A and B as a guide, mark the location of the steering dowel hole, and bore a ¾″ hole through the A-B assembly.

7 Cut the ¾″ hardwood steering dowel to length (11¾″). Hand-sand a round-over on one end of the dowel to simulate a horn button.

8 Epoxy the steering dowel into the front-axle housing (D), making sure that it's perpendicular to the housing. Rub paraffin on the bottom 2″ of steering dowel and in the ¾″ hole in the A-B assembly (the paraffin makes turning easier).

9 With a hacksaw, cut the front and rear axles to length from ½″ steel rod, where dimensioned in the Chassis Assembly drawing.

10 Attach a friction cap to one end of each axle. Now, slide a ballbearing tire, two ½″ flat washers, another tire, and the other friction cap onto each axle. Position each axle assembly in its housing with a washer and wheel at each end. Drill pilot holes and screw two mending plates to the bottom of each housing to secure the axle assemblies. With the truck carcass on its side, use a mallet to drive the friction caps tighter onto the ends of the axles. This eliminates excessive play between the rubber tires and the axle housings.

11 Referring to the appropriate Parts View drawing, mark the shape of the steering-stop block (E) on a piece of ¾″ oak, and the shape of the boom (F) on a piece of ¾″

Continued

pine. For maximum strength, lay out the boom with the grain running the length of the piece where shown in the Cutting Diagram, p. 7. Cut both pieces to shape (don't forget to cut the notch in the boom).

12 Insert the steering assembly through the hole in the A-B assembly, placing ¾" flat washers above and below the housing. Glue and screw the steering stop block (E) to the bottom of the chassis base as shown in photo A, *bottom right.* (We positioned the stop block ¼" away from the back edge of the front steering housing.)

13 Flip the chassis upright. Then, clamp a handscrew to the front tire to keep the chassis from rolling around. Drill a ³⁄₃₂" hole above the top washer to accept a cotter pin as shown in photo B, *far right.*

14 Glue the boom (F) in the notch in the chassis assembly.

Fastening the grille and firewall to the chassis

1 Using the Parts View drawing of the grille (G) as a guide, lay out and cut the grille to shape. Cut ⅛"-wide kerfs ⅛" deep in the grille front to simulate a real grille. (Using a tablesaw and the rip fence, we cut the middle kerf first. Then, we moved the fence ¼" away from the blade and cut a kerf on each side of the first, and so on.) Drill two ¼" holes where located on the drawing for the headlights that you will mount later.

2 Cut two cleats (H) to size. Drill a pilot hole through one, and screw it to the bottom of A, flush with the front. You will use the other cleat later to install the firewall (I). Now, glue and clamp the grille (G) to the front of the chassis, flush and square with the bottom of the cleat.

3 Use the Parts View drawing of the firewall (I) to mark and cut its shape on a piece of ¾" pine. Mark the position where the seat will be mounted against the firewall later, as dimensioned in the drawing. Position the firewall directly behind the grille, and check that the top profiles of both are the same. Sand as necessary to match the profiles.

4 Drill a pilot hole in the remaining cleat (H), and glue and screw it to the backside of the firewall (I). Glue and screw the firewall and cleat to the chassis assembly. (Before mounting the firewall, we used a straight piece of wood to check that the side edges of the grille, firewall, and sides of the chassis all lined up for flush-mounting of the side panels later.)

Adding the seat, side panels, splash guards, and hood

Note: For a satin-smooth paint job, we used ⅜" wood plugs over all exposed screws. See the Plug Detail on the Exploded View drawing for drill dimensions.

1 Cut the seat (J) to the size listed in the Bill of Materials. Position it in the notch in the boom (F) and against the firewall where marked. Drill pilot and plug holes, then glue and screw the seat to the boom. Glue and toe-screw the seat to the firewall, as shown in photo C.

2 Using the Side View drawing as a guide, lay out the shape of one side panel (K) on ½" pine. Cut the panel to shape with a bandsaw or jigsaw (take care when cutting the rear wheel well—you will use the remaining cutout for the splash guard [L]). Using the first panel as a template, mark and cut another panel and splash guard to shape.

3 Rout a ¼" round-over on the edges of each side panel, where shown in the Exploded View drawing. Stop the round-over where the side panels meet the hood, where

the front bumper covers the side panels, and at the wheel wells.

4 Rout a ¼" round-over on the inside edge of each splash guard (L), leaving the bottom edges square. Glue and clamp the splash guards flush with the chassis (A), centered over the rear axle.

5 Clamp the side panels against the chassis frame (make sure they are flush with the front of the grille and flush with the top of the seat). Remove the clamps, and spread glue on the mating areas of the side panels and chassis frame. Reclamp the side panels in position on the chassis frame. Drill pilot and plug holes, and screw the side panels to the chassis frame.

6 Cut the hood top (M) to size. Drill pilot and plug holes, and glue and screw the hood top to the top of the grille and firewall. Then, cut the hood side panels (N) to size, bevel-ripping the edges at 45°. (The beveled edges will protrude over the side panels and hood—you'll plane and sand these flush later.)

Drill pilot and plug holes, and then glue and screw the hood side panels to the grille and firewall as shown in photo D, *below.*

7 Using a block plane, plane the protruding edges of the hood side panels almost flush with the side panels (K) and hood top (M). Now, sand the hood panels flush.

8 Rout a ¼″ round-over along the front edge of the hood, hood side panels, and side panels, again stopping where you will attach the bumper later.

9 Cut ⅜″ pine plugs with a plug cutter, or cut lengths of ⅜″ dowel. Plug all the screw holes, and sand the plugs flush.

10 Fill all gaps with wood putty and finish-sand the chassis assembly. (We usually finish-sand just before we apply the finish, but it's easier in this instance to sand before attaching the bumper.)

Now for the front bumper, steering wheel, and headlights

1 Cut the front bumper (O) to size. Rout a ¼″ round-over along its front edges and finish-sand. Drill pilot and plug holes, and glue and

screw the bumper to the front of the grille, with the bottom edge of both being flush. Plug the holes and sand the plugs.

2 Using a compass, mark the 6″-diameter steering wheel (P) and cut it to shape. Drill a ¾″ hole through the center of the steering wheel (use the same centerpoint you used to mark the circle). Sand out the saw marks along the outside edge of the steering wheel, and rout a ¼″ round-over along the top and bottom edges. Finish-sand the steering wheel.

3 Using a holesaw or circle cutter, cut two 2½″-diameter headlights (Q). Glue a 1½″ length of ¼″ dowel stock into the center hole in each headlight, keeping one end of the dowel flush with the front surface of the headlights. After the glue dries, chuck the dowel into your drill press. Turn the drill press on, and sand a round-over on the front edge of each headlight.

Getting ready for the road

1 Remove the tire/axle assemblies from the housings (C, D), and remove the steering dowel/front axle housing from the chassis.

Note: Paint the tow truck the "easy way", or spend a little more time, money, and paint for the "deluxe treatment". Either way, use an exterior oil-based enamel paint for a durable, long-wearing finish.

The easy way. Apply a coat of sanding sealer to all the wood parts (including the steering wheel and headlights). Follow with two coats of exterior enamel.

The deluxe paint job. We stained wood-grained areas on each side panel (see the opening photo). Then, after letting the stain dry thoroughly, we applied a coat of sanding sealer to the entire truck, steering wheel, and headlights. After the sanding sealer dried, we masked off everything except the undercarriage and bumper, and spray-painted them black. We also painted the steering wheel and steering dowel/front axle housing (both are unattached) black.

(When you paint the steering dowel, mask off the spot where the steering wheel will be mounted. When painting the steering wheel, fill the ¾″ hole with paper to keep paint out and to ensure good adhesion to the steering dowel later.)

Later, we masked off the undercarriage, the previously stained area on the side panels, and the bumper. Then, we spray-painted the body yellow and the headlights white. Finally, we fast-talked an artist friend into doing a little custom lettering.

2 After the paint has dried, reattach the axles to C and D using the mending plates. Place a washer onto the steering dowel. Insert the steering dowel through the chassis assembly (A-B), add another washer, and push the dowel through the hole in the hood. Insert a cotter pin into the hole in the steering dowel, and flange its end to lock the steering dowel to the chassis.

3 Glue the headlights in place in the ¼″ holes in the front of the grille. Turn the truck on its side, and glue the steering wheel onto the steering dowel (this keeps the steering wheel in place and prevents epoxy from dripping onto the steering dowel or body).

4 Twist a screw eye into the end of the boom. Tie a short length of nylon cord to the screw eye, and attach an "S" hook to the other end of the cord. Using a pliers, force the end of the "S" hook closed on the nylon cord.

Buying Guide

● **Plug cutter.** Catalog no. W511. For the current price, contact Meisel Hardware Spec., P.O. Box 70, Mound, MN, 55364-0070. Or call 800-441-9870 or 612-471-8550 to order.

● **Tropical hardwood epoxy.** Slow-set epoxy, one pint can of resin, one pint of hardener, and instructions. For the current price, contact Smith & Co., 5100 Channel Ave., Richmond, CA 94804. Call 800-234-0330. ♣

Produced by: Marlen Kemmet
Project Design: Kim Downing
Photographs: Bob Calmer; Jim Kascoutas

THE BOARD OF

A fun-to-make learning toy that teaches

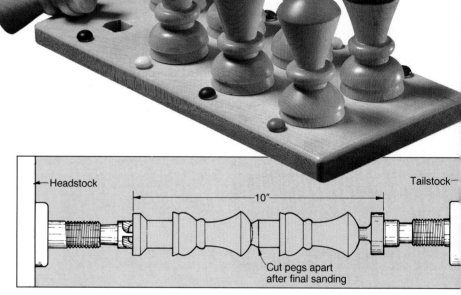

Children have a hard time keeping their hands off this learning toy. The challenge of mating bright colors and different shapes will certainly captivate your favorite preschoolers, too.

Headstock —
10"
Tailstock —
Cut pegs apart
after final sanding

The board comes first

1 Rip and crosscut a piece of ¾"-thick maple to 5½" wide by 12½" long. Mark the locations for the wooden buttons and pegs where shown on the Board Drawing on the opposite page.
2 Drill ⅜" holes ¼" deep for the buttons where marked. Then, drill the ⅝", ¾", ⅞", and 1" peg holes.
3 Using carbon paper or a photocopy, center and transfer the full-sized peg-bottom patterns over the remaining four centerpoints. Drill blade start holes, and cut the openings to shape with a scroll-saw or coping saw.

And now, for the pegs

1 Crosscut a 2" maple turning square to 10" long. If you don't have stock this size, laminate thinner stock. (We found it easier to turn identical-shaped pegs if we turned two at a time.)
2 Draw diagonals on both ends to find centers, and mount the turning square between centers on the lathe. Start the lathe, and turn the square round.

3 Using a photocopy or carbon paper, transfer the full-sized template pattern shown on the opposite page to posterboard or hardboard, and cut the template to shape.
4 Using the drawing *above* for reference, turn the pegs to shape. (We used a ⅜" gouge and a parting tool.) Turn the tenoned base of four of the pegs to fit into the ⅝", ¾", ⅞", and 1" hole openings (we frequently stopped the lathe and measured the round tenons with an outside calipers to ensure a good fit into their mating holes). Next, turn four pegs leaving the tenons 1" in diameter. Sand the pegs smooth and finish cutting between the pegs with a bandsaw or handsaw where shown on the drawing.

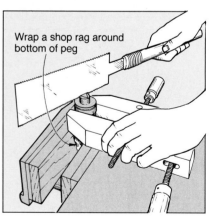

Wrap a shop rag around bottom of peg

5 Trace the four patterns onto the bottom surface of the 1" diameter tenons. As shown in the drawing *above,* wrap a cloth around the peg to prevent marring it, and clamp it steady. Use a dovetail saw to cut each tenon to shape.

EDUCATION
colors and shapes

Add the finish, and call the little ones

1 Sand the board smooth. Apply a clear finish to the board and pegs. (Before applying the finish, we stuck a 1"-long piece of ⅜" dowel stock in each ⅜" hole to prevent finish from running into the button holes. We removed the dowels after the finish dried.) Steel-wool the top of the pegs and paint them (we used enamel).

2 Paint the wood buttons to match the peg tops. Glue and tap the pegs into the ⅜" holes (we used a rubber mallet to prevent chipping the painted tops of the buttons). 🌳

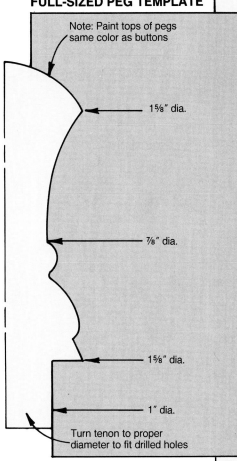

FULL-SIZED PEG TEMPLATE

Note: Paint tops of pegs same color as buttons

1⅝" dia.

⅞" dia.

1⅝" dia.

1" dia.

Turn tenon to proper diameter to fit drilled holes

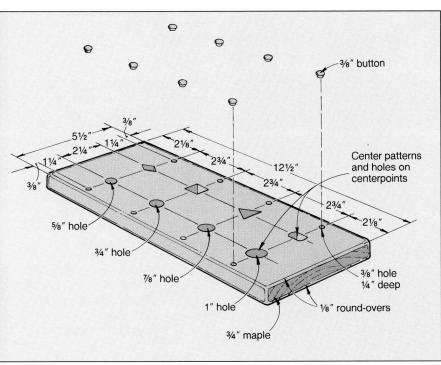

⅜" button

5½"
3⅛"
2¼"
1¼"
1¼"
⅜"
2⅛"
2¾"
12½"
2¾"
2¾"
2⅛"

Center patterns and holes on centerpoints

⅝" hole
¾" hole
⅞" hole
1" hole
¾" maple

⅜" hole ¼" deep
⅛" round-overs

Patterns require a 1" tenon on end of pegs

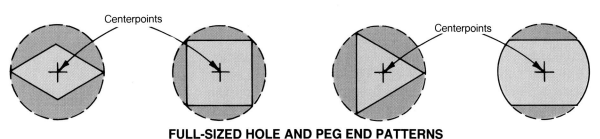

Centerpoints

Centerpoints

FULL-SIZED HOLE AND PEG END PATTERNS

Project Design: Jerome Kobishop   Photographs: Hopkins Associates   Ilustrations: Kim Downing; Bill Zaun

Note: See the Buying Guide on page 17 for our source of plans for the dollhouse furniture shown.

Call the framing crew to erect the walls

1 Using the dimensions on the Parts View drawing on page 14, lay out the dollhouse front (A), side walls (B), partitions (C), and second floor (D) onto a 4×8 sheet of ¼″-thick birch plywood. Refer to the Cutting Diagram shown on page 15 for positioning the pieces on the plywood. Be sure to mark the window openings, door openings, and slots on the six pieces as you lay them out.

2 With a utility knife and a straightedge, score all of the lines you just marked. Doing this will minimize splintering when you cut out the pieces. Using a jigsaw fitted with a fine-toothed plywood-cutting blade, cut the parts to shape.

3 Drill blade-start holes, and cut the openings and slots to size. Check the fit of the mating parts in the slots; adjust if necessary.

4 Cut the roof (E) to the size listed in the Bill of Materials.

And now, add the trim

1 Cut the columns (F), window shutters (G, H), and door shutters (I) to the sizes listed in the Bill of Materials. Sand the edges smooth.

2 Glue and tape the columns and shutters in place (we used spring clamps and masking tape to hold the pieces until the glue dried). Note the position of the outside columns where shown on the Hinge Detail in the lower right-hand corner on the opposite page.

3 Cut the front door (J) to size, and set it aside for now.

Assemble the pieces for home sweet home

1 Insert the partitions (C) into the slots in the second floor (D).

Continued

Readers who tour the WOOD® offices love to peek at projects we're preparing. When Terry Edens of Davenport, Iowa visited us, and spotted our dollhouse he said, "Boy, that's just what I've been looking for! My kids have said that the graddaughters don't have room for a dollhouse that they'd have to keep around all the time. But this is perfect. When can I start building?" Well Terry, this knockdown unit should fit the bill. When playtime is over, all the pieces fit neatly into the handy carrying case.

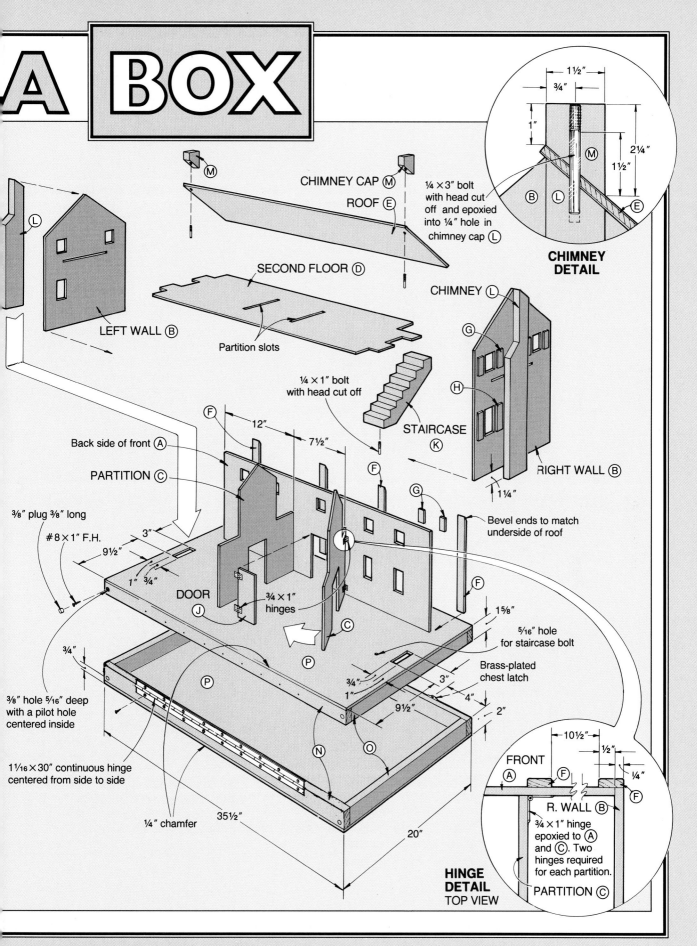

A BOX

CHIMNEY CAP ⓜ

ROOF Ⓔ

SECOND FLOOR Ⓓ

Partition slots

¼ × 3″ bolt with head cut off and epoxied into ¼″ hole in chimney cap Ⓛ

CHIMNEY DETAIL

1½″
¾″
1″
2¼″
1½″
Ⓜ
Ⓑ Ⓛ Ⓔ

LEFT WALL Ⓑ

¼ × 1″ bolt with head cut off

STAIRCASE Ⓚ

CHIMNEY Ⓛ
Ⓖ
Ⓗ

RIGHT WALL Ⓑ

1¼″

Ⓕ
12″
7½″

Back side of front Ⓐ

PARTITION Ⓒ

Ⓕ

Ⓖ

Bevel ends to match underside of roof

⅜″ plug ⅜″ long

#8 × 1″ F.H.

3″

9½″

1″ ¾″

DOOR
Ⓙ

¾ × 1″ hinges

Ⓒ

Ⓕ

5/16″ hole for staircase bolt

1⅝″

Brass-plated chest latch

¾″ ⎯
1″
3″
4″
9½″
2″

Ⓟ

¾″

⅜″ hole 5/16″ deep with a pilot hole centered inside

1 1/16 × 30″ continuous hinge centered from side to side

¼″ chamfer

35½″

Ⓝ Ⓞ

20″

HINGE DETAIL
TOP VIEW

10½″
½″
¼″

FRONT
Ⓐ Ⓕ

R. WALL Ⓑ
Ⓕ

¾ × 1″ hinge epoxied to Ⓐ and Ⓒ. Two hinges required for each partition.

PARTITION Ⓒ

DOLLHOUSE

PARTS VIEW

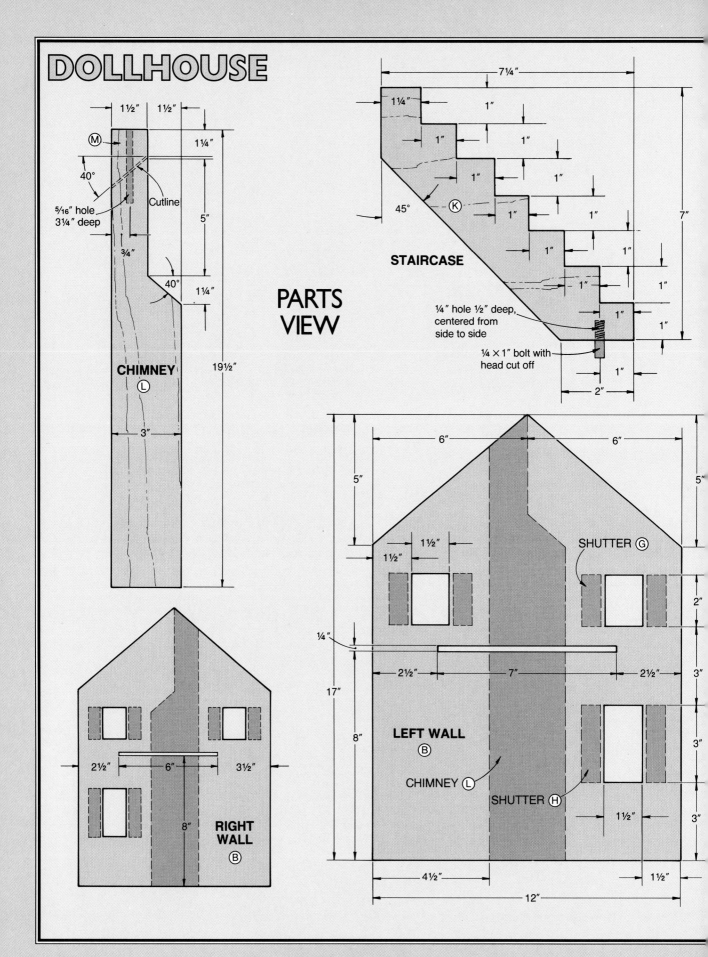

CHIMNEY Ⓛ

M

40°

1½" 1½"

1¼"

5/16" hole
3¼" deep

Cutline

¾"

40°

5"

1¼"

19½"

3"

STAIRCASE

7¼"

1¼"

1"

1"

1"

1"

1"

1"

1"

1"

1"

1"

1"

1"

45°

Ⓚ

7"

¼" hole ½" deep,
centered from
side to side

¼ × 1" bolt with
head cut off

2"

RIGHT WALL Ⓑ

2½"   6"   3½"

8"

LEFT WALL Ⓑ

6"   6"

5"

5"

1½"

1½"

SHUTTER Ⓖ

2"

¼"

2½"   7"   2½"

3"

17"

8"

CHIMNEY Ⓛ

SHUTTER Ⓗ

3"

3"

1½"

4½"   1½"

12"

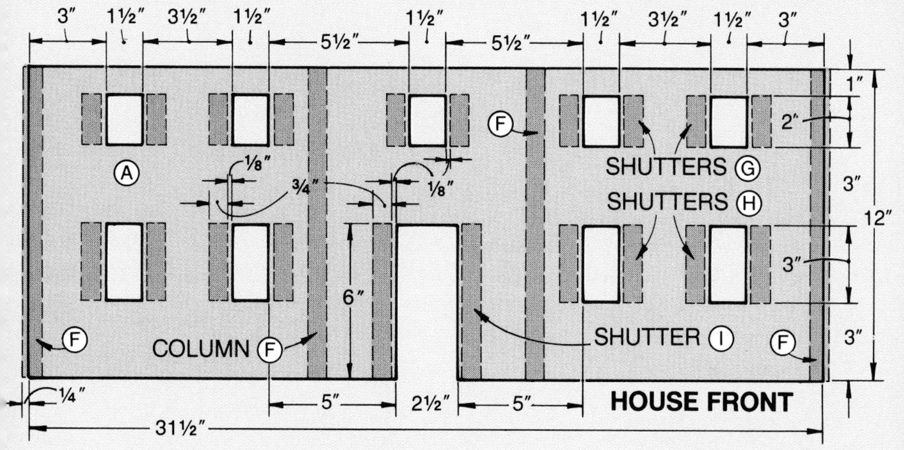

3″
1½″
3½″
1½″
5½″
1½″
5½″
1½″
3½″
1½″
3″
1″
2″
3″
12″
3″
3″
A
F
⅛″
¾″
⅛″
SHUTTERS G
SHUTTERS H
6″
SHUTTER I
F
COLUMN F
F
¼″
5″
2½″
5″
HOUSE FRONT
31½″

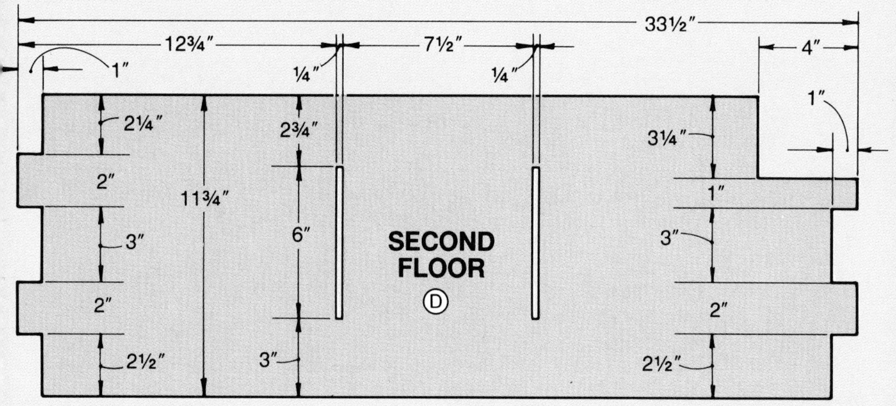

33½″
12¾″
7½″
4″
1″
¼″
¼″
1″
2¼″
2¾″
3¼″
2″
11¾″
1″
3″
6″
SECOND FLOOR
D
3″
2″
2″
2½″
3″
2½″

PARTITIONS

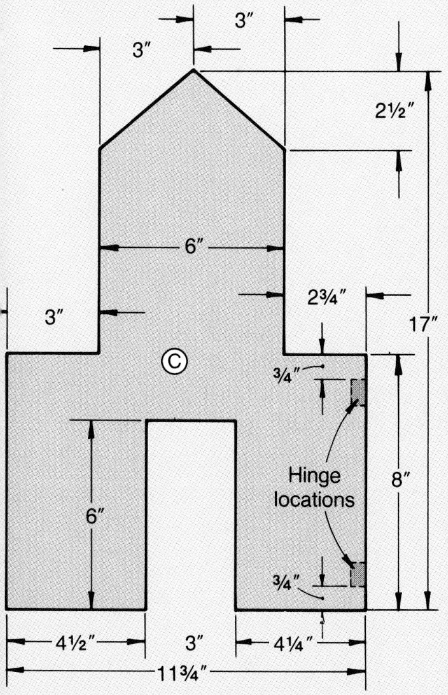

3″
3″
2½″
6″
2¾″
3″
17″
C
¾″
Hinge locations
8″
6″
¾″
4½″
3″
4¼″
11¾″

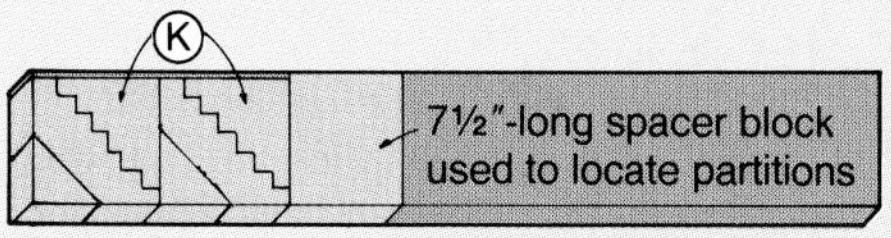

K
7½″-long spacer block used to locate partitions

1½ × 7¼ (2 × 8) × 48″ Fir, Pine, or Spruce

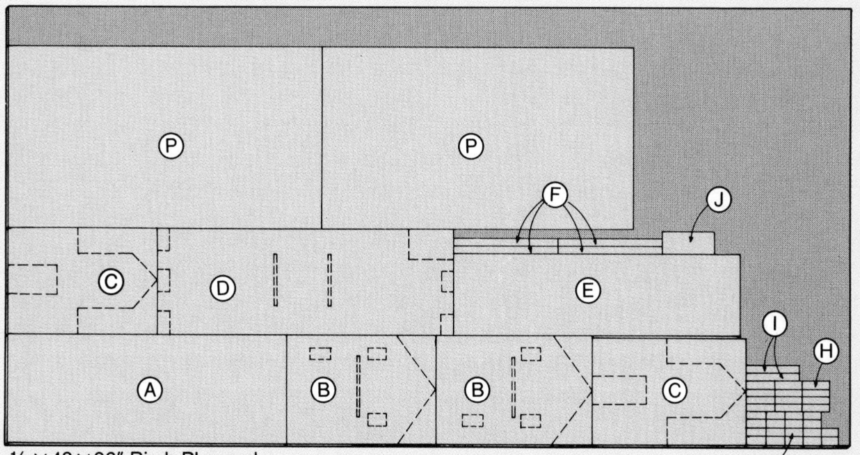

P
P
F
J
C
D
E
A
B
B
C
I
H
G

¼ × 48 × 96″ Birch Plywood

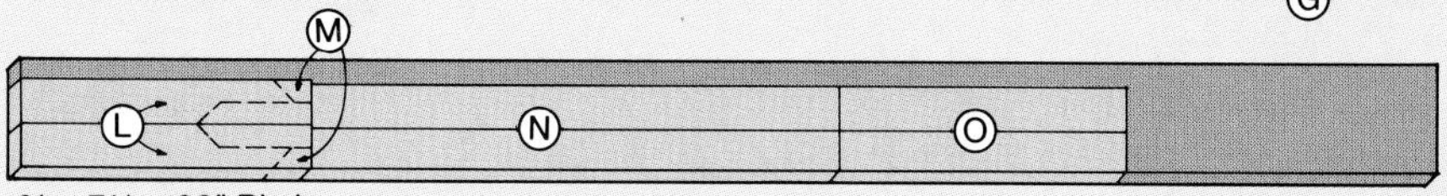

M
L
N
O

¾ × 7¼ × 96″ Birch

Bill of Materials

Part		Finished Size* T	W	L	Matl.	Qty.
DOLLHOUSE						
A	front	¼″	12″	31½″	BP	1
B	walls	¼″	12″	17″	BP	2
C	partitions	¼″	11¾″	17″	BP	2
D	second floor	¼″	11¾″	33½″	BP	1
E	roof	¼″	9″	33½″	BP	1
F	columns	¼″	¾″	12″	BP	4
G	shutters	¼″	¾″	2″	BP	18
H	shutters	¼″	¾″	3″	BP	12
I	door shutters	¼″	¾″	6″	BP	2
J	door	¼″	2⁷⁄₁₆″	5¹⁵⁄₁₆″	BP	1
K	staircase	3″	7″	7¼″	LF	1
L	chimneys	¾″	3″	18¼″	B	2
M	chimney caps	¾″	1½″	2¼″	B	2
STORAGE CASE						
N	case sides	¾″	3¼″	35½″	B	2
O	case ends	¾″	3¼″	18½″	B	2
P	case panels	¼″	20″	35½″	BP	2

Material Key: BP-birch plywood
LF-laminated fir

Supplies: quick-set epoxy, three pair of ¾ × 1″ brass hinges (Stanley part no. CD5302), one pair of brass-plated chest latches with screws (Stanley part no. CD5365), 1¹⁄₁₆ × 30″ continuous hinge with screws (Stanley part no. SC311), #8 × 1″ flathead wood screws, ¼ × 3″ hex-head bolt, ¼ × 1″ hex-head bolt, paint.

Continued

DOLLHOUSE

2 Position the front piece (A) face down on your workbench. Place the partition/second-floor assembly on the back side of the front piece, with the ends flush where shown on the drawing on the opposite page. Make sure, too, that the bottom edges of the partitions are flush with the bottom edge of the front piece. Cut a spacer to length, and clamp it between the partitions where shown in the drawing. (The spacer helps keep the partitions square to the front piece.) Check that the partitions are square with the front piece, and then tape the partitions to the spacer.

3 Discard the screws packaged with the ¾×1″ brass hinges. Then, epoxy the hinges to the front piece. (We used quick-set epoxy, and lightly sanded the hinge surfaces for better adhesion to the epoxy.) Later, epoxy the other leaf of each hinge to the partitions.

4 Repeat the process in Step 3 *above* to epoxy the front-door hinges to the front piece (A) and the door (J).

Two steps make a staircase

1 Cut two pieces of 2×8 to 7″ wide by 7¼″ long. (When cutting the pieces to width, we ripped both edges of the 2×8 to get rid of the rounded-off corners of the board.) Glue and clamp the pieces together face to face for the staircase lamination (K). Using the dimensions on the Parts View Drawing and a combination square, mark the steps on the 2×8 lamination. With a bandsaw, cut the staircase to shape.

2 Drill a ¼″ hole ½″ deep in the stair bottom where shown on the Parts View Drawing. Cut off the head of a ¼×1″ bolt, and epoxy it into the hole in the staircase. See the staircase on the Parts View Drawing for reference.

No mason necessary for these chimneys!

1 Transfer the dimensions for the chimneys (L, M) to ¾″ birch. (See the Parts View Drawing for dimensions.) Cut each chimney to shape.

2 Draw diagonals to find center, and then drill a ⁵⁄₁₆″ hole 3¼″ deep in the top center of each chimney. (Again, see the chimney on the Parts View Drawing for reference.) Mark the angled cutlines, and cut each chimney cap (M) from the chimney (L).

3 Glue one chimney to each wall (B) where shown on the Parts View Drawing.

Next, build the case to house the home

1 Cut the case sides (N) and ends (O) to size from ¾″ birch stock.

2 With the surfaces flush, glue and clamp the sides and ends together, checking for square.

3 Measure the length and width of the case frame, and cut the two case side panels (P) to size from ¼″ plywood. With the edges and ends flush, glue and clamp the side panels to the frame. Later, sand edges of the plywood flush with the edges of the frame. Rout or sand a ¼″ chamfer along the plywood edges where shown on the Exploded-View Drawing.

4 Drill screw holes and strengthen the joints with #8×1″ flathead wood screws where shown on the Exploded-View Drawing. Plug the holes and sand the plugs flush.

5 Locate and mark the chimney-hole locations onto the plywood-case top where shown on the Exploded-View Drawing. Drill blade-start holes, and cut the chimney slots to shape.

6 Raise your tablesaw blade ⅞″ above the surface of the saw table. Position the fence 2″ from the inside edge of the blade. As shown in the photo *above right,* cut the case in two. (To keep the saw kerfs from collapsing, we taped ⅛″ spacers in each kerf after cutting it.) After making the final cut, remove the tape and spacers.

7 Position the case halves together with the edges and ends flush. Center the 1¹⁄₁₆×30″ continuous hinge over the joint line along one edge, centered from side to side, and screw it in place.

Position the tablesaw fence, raise the blade, and cut one edge at a time to saw the storage case in two.

8 Attach the latches to the case where shown on the Exploded-View Drawing.

Complete the construction

1 Fit the dollhouse onto the case so the chimneys slip into the chimney holes in the case panel (P).

2 Position the staircase against the backside of the front (A) and flush against the right wall (B). Use a pencil to mark the location for the bolt-mounting hole on the case top (P). Remove the staircase, and drill a ⁵⁄₁₆″ hole where marked.

3 Tape the roof (E) to the top of the end walls (see the Chimney Detail accompanying the Exploded-View Drawing for location). Mark the location of the chimney caps (M), and then glue and tape them to the top of the roof squarely over the chimney bottoms (L).

4 Remove the roof from the assembly. Using the previously drilled hole in each chimney cap as a guide, drill a hole through the roof at each chimney cap as shown in the photo on the opposite page.

5 Cut off the head of two ¼×3″ hex head bolts, and epoxy one bolt into the hole in each chimney cap (M). See the Chimney Detail accompanying the Exploded-View

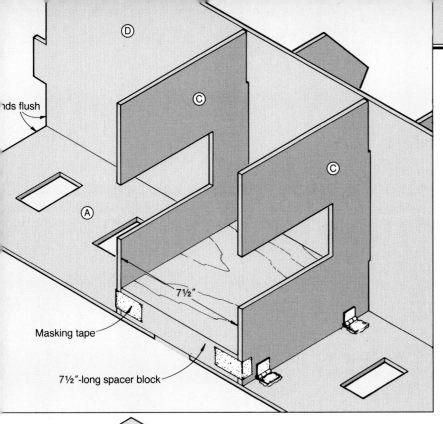

ds flush

Ⓓ

Ⓒ

Ⓒ

Ⓐ

7½"

Masking tape

7½"-long spacer block

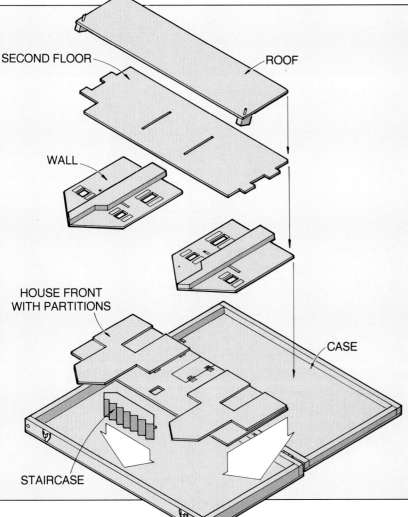

SECOND FLOOR

ROOF

WALL

HOUSE FRONT
WITH PARTITIONS

CASE

STAIRCASE

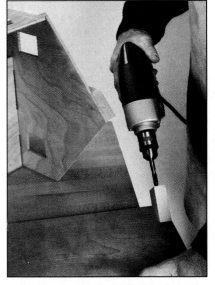

Using the previously drilled hole in the chimney cap as a guide, drill a ¼″ hole through the roof.

Drawing for reference. (We found that using a bolt is much stronger than a dowel, which has a tendency to break with heavy use.)

Call the house painters

1 Sand the parts and remove the latches and continuous hinge.
2 Paint the pieces with semigloss enamel. (For our house and case, we applied Rust-Oleum Wood Saver paints. After the first coat dried, we brushed the end grain with an extra coat. After that dried, we repainted all the surfaces.)
3 Now, add the trim lines on the chimney (we used a medium-point felt-tipped marker for this).
4 Attach the hardware. To store the pieces inside the carrying case, see the drawing at *left*.

Buying Guide
● **Dollhouse furniture plans.** Catalog no. W511, For the current price, contact Meisel Hardware Spec., P.O. Box 70, Mound, MN, 55364-0070. Or call 800-441-9870 or 612-471-8550 to order. 🌲

Project Design: Dave Ashe; James R. Downing
Photographs: Hopkins Associates; Jim Kascoutas
Illustrations: Kim Downing; Bill Zaun

PLOW-TIME
TRACTOR

F Finally, a stylish toy that you don't have to run out and buy wheels for. In fact, with just a circle cutter, drill press, and router, you can fashion these handsome wheels in a jiffy from scrap stock. Plus, this little tractor's built so tough, it'll spend it's time plowing imaginary fields and not on the woodshop workbench waiting for repairs.

The chassis and body parts come first

1 Cut the chassis (A), axle block (B), hitch (C), and seat (D) to the sizes listed in the Bill of Materials. Mark and cut the radius on the rear of the hitch where shown on the Exploded View drawing. Now, drill a ⅜″ hole through the hitch where shown.

2 Glue and clamp the axle block and hitch to the bottom of the chassis where shown on the Hitch Detail. Glue the seat flush with the back edge of the chassis.

3 Mark the centerpoints and drill four axle holes ¾″ deep in the chassis where located on the Exploded View drawing.

Note: Measure the diameter of your toy pegs before drilling the axle holes. We've found some that require ⁵⁄₁₆″ holes for a snug fit and others needed ⅜″ holes. Test-drill holes in scrap first.

4 Cut the grille and firewall (E) and motor (F) to size (we lami-

nated two ¾″ pieces for the motor). Drill four ⁵⁄₁₆″ holes in the motor where shown on the drawing. Using a handsaw, cut kerfs in the grille front where shown on the drawing. Glue and clamp the parts to the chassis.

5 Transfer the full-sized hood (G) pattern to the edge of a piece of ½″ stock 2½″ wide by 2¾″ long. Cut it to shape. Glue the hood to the tractor assembly.

6 Sand ⅛″ round-overs on the tractor body where shown.

7 Using the side view of the backrest (H) for reference, cut the piece to shape and sand round-overs on all but the bottom edges. Glue and clamp the backrest to the seat.

8 Trim four ⁵⁄₁₆ × 1⁹⁄₁₆″ axle pegs to ⅜″ long, and glue them in the holes drilled in the motor.

9 Mark the radius, and then bandsaw the steering wheel (I) to shape from ¼″ stock. Cut a piece of ¼″ dowel to 1⅛″ long for the steering wheel rod, and drill a ¼″

hole in the tractor where shown on the Hole detail. Glue the wheel to the dowel.

	Bill of Materials					
	Parts	**Finished Size**			**Matl.**	**Qty.**
		T	**W**	**L**		
A	chassis	¾″	2½″	5½″	W	1
B	axle block	¾″	½″	2½″	W	1
C	hitch	¾″	½″	5½″	W	1
D	seat	¾″	1½″	2½″	W	1
E	grille & firewall	½″	2½″	1¼″	W	2
F	motor	1½″	1¼″	1¾″	LW	1
G	hood	½″	2½″	2¾″	W	1
H	backrest	½″	1⅛″	2″	W	1
I	steering wheel	¼″	1¼″ diam.		W	1
J	front wheels	¾″	2¼″ diam.		W	2
K	back wheels	¾″	3½″ diam.		W	2

Material Key: W-walnut, LW-laminated walnut
Supplies: ¼″ dowel stock, 8—⁵⁄₁₆ × 1⁹⁄₁₆″ axle pegs, finish.

Add some wheels for traction

1 With a circle cutter, cut the 2¼"-diameter front wheels (J) to shape. Then, counterbore a 1" hole ¼" deep on the outside face of each wheel.

2 Using the rear Wheel drawing for reference, lay out the rear wheels (K) on ¾" stock, and drill four ¾" holes in each where shown. Reset the circle cutter, and cut a pair of 3½"-diameter rear wheels to shape.

3 Redrill the ¼" pilot hole in each of the four wheels to ⅜".

4 Rout ¼" round-overs on the outside edges of wheels. (To do this, we cut a V-shaped notch in a 20"-long piece of scrap stock and clamped it to our router table as shown in the photo at *right*. This enabled us to rout the wheels

while keeping our fingers safely away from the router bit.) Now, remove the fence and round-over the edges of the ¾" holes.

Apply the finish, and head for the north 40

1 Sand the tractor smooth.

2 Add finish to the wheels, steering wheel, and tractor body, being careful not to get any finish in the tractor body, axle, or steering wheel holes. (To achieve the finish shown, we sanded the bare wood with 280-grit paper. Then, applied Deft, an aerosol lacquer, and lightly sanded it with 280-grit paper. After applying the next coat, we rubbed it with 0000 steel wool.) Glue and pin the wheels to the tractor body with the 5⁄16×1 9⁄16" axle pegs. Mount the steering wheel. 🌳

For safety, use a router with a V-shaped notch when routing the wheels.

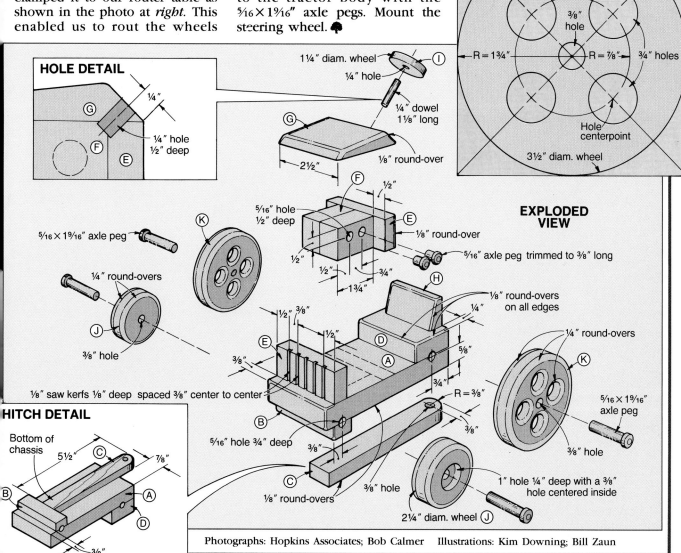

HOLE DETAIL

REAR WHEEL Ⓚ

EXPLODED VIEW

HITCH DETAIL

Photographs: Hopkins Associates; Bob Calmer   Illustrations: Kim Downing; Bill Zaun

THE RED BARON, JR. *Happy*

With your supervision, a youngster probably can handle most of the layout, cutting, and assembly of this high-flyin' project—depending, of course on his or her skill level and age.

Landings
TOY AIRPLANE

First you make the fuselage, wing, and stabilizer

1 Rip a piece of pine to 1½" square. Measure 5¼" from one end and cut the fuselage (A) to length.

2 Using the full-sized patterns on page 23 and the drawing *below* for reference, lay out and mark the

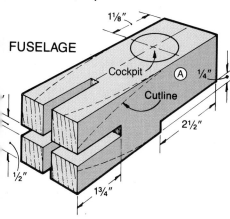

FUSELAGE
1⅛"
Cockpit
(A) ¼"
Cutline
2½"
½"
1¾"

notches needed to hold the elevator (B) and the rudder (C). Do the same for the rabbet that will accept the wing. Then, using a bandsaw or a handsaw, chisel and mallet, cut the notches to size. And with a bandsaw or a dado blade mounted in your radial-arm saw or tablesaw, cut the 2½" rabbet ¼" deep in the underside of the fuselage.

3 Mark the location of the cockpit, again using the drawing *above* as reference. Drill a 1¼" hole ⅜" deep where the two lines intersect. Now, drill a 1" hole through the center of the first hole and through the entire thickness of the fuselage, using a scrap board below the piece being drilled to prevent chip-out.

4 Draw diagonal lines from corner to corner on the front of the fuselage (A) to mark the centerpoint for the prop-shaft hole. With a ¼" bit, drill ½" deep into the front of the fuselage where marked.

5 Using the pattern on page 23 as a guide, mark the taper on the tail end of the fuselage. Cut the taper to shape with a bandsaw or jigsaw. Now, round-over the square edges the length of the fuselage with a block plane or wood rasp.

6 Using carbon paper, transfer the shape of the rudder (B), elevator (C), and wing (D) onto ¼" stock. Remember to trace the notches and the strut holes. Cut the parts to shape, then cut the notches in B and C. (We resawed ¾" pine and walnut to form the ¼" thick stock.)

7 To form the strut holes, drill two ¼" holes side by side. Cut the rectangular holes to shape with a mallet and chisel as shown in the photo *below*.

8 Sand all curves smooth, and sand a slight chamfer on any sharp edges. Test the fit of B and C into the notches in the fuselage. (Some filing and sanding may be necessary for a good fit.)

Now, let's cut the propeller parts

1 Using a circle cutter on the drill press, cut the motor (E) and nose cone (F) to shape. Sand a slight round-over on the front edge of both pieces. (To sand the round-

over and other round biplane parts smooth, we mounted the parts [E, F, I] on ¼" dowel stock. Then, we mounted the dowel in the chuck on our drill press, turned the drill on at a low speed, and sanded the parts smooth.)

2 Using carbon paper, transfer the shape of the propeller (G) to ¼" stock, and cut to shape. Drill a 5⁄16" hole through the center of the prop, and ¼" holes through the center of the motor and nose cone.

3 Cut the prop shaft to length (1¾") from ¼" dowel stock.

Here's how to guarantee a smooth landing

1 Once again using the full-sized patterns, transfer the shape of both struts (H) onto ¼" stock. Cut the struts to shape, stick them together with double-faced tape, and drill a 5⁄16" hole through both for the axles. Check for a tight fit of the struts through the strut holes in the wings, and sand if necessary.

2 Use a small-diameter rasp or a ¼" dowel with sandpaper wrapped around it to form the groove for the guns on the top end of the struts as shown in the photo *below*.

Continued

3 Using a circle cutter, cut the two wheels (I) to size (1¼″ diameter). Drill a ¼″ hole in the center of each. You can also buy 1¼″-diameter wooden toy wheels, which also have ¼″ axle holes.

4 Cut the wheel axle to length (4¼″) from ¼″ dowel stock. Using the same size of dowel stock, cut the two guns to length. Drill a ⅛″ hole ¼″ deep centered in the front end of each gun.

TOY AIRPLANE

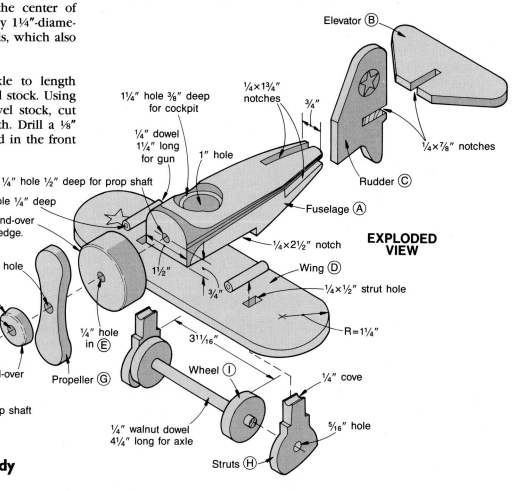

Elevator Ⓑ

¼×1¾″ notches

¾″

¼×⅞″ notches

Rudder Ⓒ

1¼″ hole ⅜″ deep for cockpit

¼″ dowel 1¼″ long for gun

1″ hole

¼″ hole ½″ deep for prop shaft

⅛″ hole ¼″ deep

Sand a slight round-over on the front edge.

Fuselage Ⓐ

¼×2½″ notch

EXPLODED VIEW

⁵⁄₁₆″ hole

Nose cone Ⓕ

¼″ hole

¼″ hole in Ⓔ

1½″

¾″

Wing Ⓓ

¼×½″ strut hole

Round-over

Propeller Ⓖ

3¹¹⁄₁₆″

R=1¼″

¼″ walnut dowel 1¾″ long for prop shaft

Wheel Ⓘ

¼″ cove

¼″ walnut dowel 4¼″ long for axle

⁵⁄₁₆″ hole

Struts Ⓗ

You're almost ready for takeoff

I Sand all the parts smooth, sand all sharp edges. (While most projects are sanded after completion, it is much easier to sand this one before gluing. It takes more time to try and sand around all the parts, especially the moving ones, later.)

2 Glue the rudder, then the elevator in the tail end of the fuselage. Glue and clamp the wing to the underside of the fuselage.

3 Attach the motor (E), propeller (G), and then the nose cone (F) to the fuselage (A) with the ¼″-walnut dowel. Glue the motor to the body, and glue the nose cone to the dowel. (Be careful not to get any glue on the prop so that it can spin freely on the ¼″ dowel.)

Bill of Materials				
Part	**Finished Size**			Material	Qty.
	T	W	L		
A	1½″	1½″	5¼″	pine	1
B	¼″	1¾″	4⅛″	pine	1
C	¼″	1¾″	3½″	walnut	1
D	¼″	2½″	8½″	pine	1
E	¾″	2″ diam.		pine	1
F	¼″	1″ diam.		pine	1
G	¼″	1″	3½″	walnut	1
H	¼″	1½″	2″	walnut	2
I	¼″	1¼″diam.		pine	2

Supplies: ¼″ walnut dowel, ¼″ birch dowel, tung oil, pilot figure (you can use a Fisher-Price Air Pilot or order a wood "person" from most toy-part catalogs), adhesive-backed decals and colored tape.

4 Glue the wheels (I) in place on the axle. After the glue dries, fit, but don't glue, the struts (H) onto the axle. Position and glue the struts in place through the wings. Finally, glue the guns into the coves on top of the struts.

5 If you want your airplane to look exactly like ours, attach colored tape and decals. (We found the colored tape at a local hardware store and decals at a hobby shop.)

6 Finish the entire airplane (we used several coats of tung oil), and you're ready to fly. ♣

Project Design: Kim Downing
Photographs: Hopkins Associates
Illustrations: Kim Downing, Bill Zaun

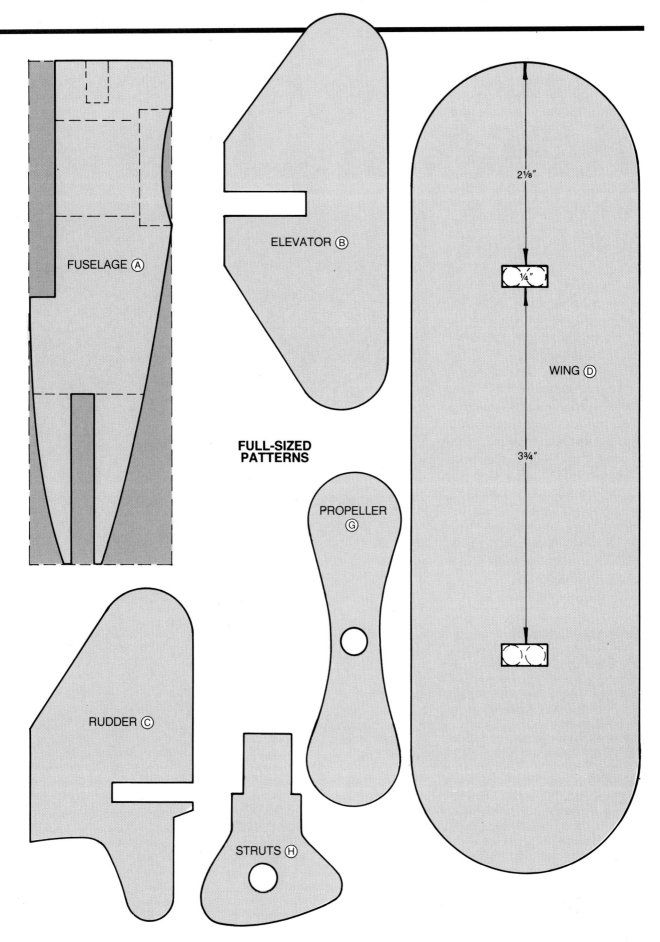

FUSELAGE Ⓐ

ELEVATOR Ⓑ

WING Ⓓ

2⅛″

¼″

3¾″

FULL-SIZED
PATTERNS

PROPELLER
Ⓖ

RUDDER Ⓒ

STRUTS Ⓗ

Thoroughbred Rocking Horse

From Merry Olde England

If you want to see a little tyke's eyes light up, give this rocking horse as a present. It's lightweight, yet sturdy—and very huggable.

Much like the seventeenth-century original in the Museum of London, our version is made safer by the projections at the front and rear of each rocker. The "stops" prevent energetic riders from tipping too far forward or backward while they whoop it up in the saddle. Plus, the dowel and wooden ball foot and hand holds provide support for young feet and hands.

Ready the rockers

1 From ¾" cherry, rip three pieces 4¼×76". Edge-join the pieces together, clamping scrap stock across the pieces to keep them flat. Scrape off the excess glue once a tough skin has formed.

2 Crosscut the lamination in half to form the blanks for the rockers (A). With a tablesaw, bevel-rip the top edge of each rocker piece at 15°. Then, use double-faced tape to stick the two rockers together with the high edges (points) of the bevels together and flush.

3 With a ruler and straightedge, lay out 1" squares on a large piece of paper to form a grid pattern measuring 13×36". Use spray adhesive on the back of the grid paper to attach it to the taped-together rocker pieces.

4 Using the Rocker Grid drawing on the opposite page as a guide, mark the points where the rocker outline crosses each grid line to lay out the front and rear stops and top 3" of the rocker. Connect the points to transfer the shape of the rocker stops onto the grid paper. Mark the location of the stirrup opening as well as the footrest hole and screw holes (for part C) where shown on the drawing. To form the rocker bottom, drive 1" brads into the grid where shown on the drawing. Clamp a flexible strip of wood to the brads and trace along the inside edge of the strip as shown in the photo *above right*.

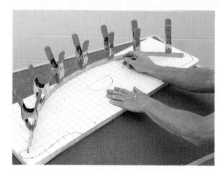

5 With the rockers still taped together, cut them to shape. Drill a ½" blade access hole through the marked stirrup opening; then cut the opening to shape with a jigsaw or scrollsaw.

6 Drill three ⁵⁄₃₂" holes through both rockers for later mounting of the brace (C). Then, drill a ⁵⁄₃₂"

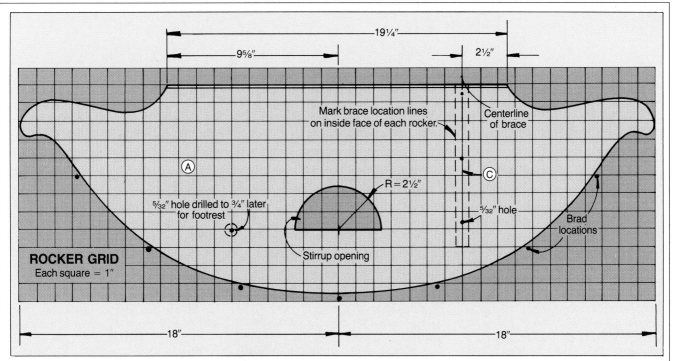

ROCKER GRID
Each square = 1"

19¼"

9⅝"

2½"

Mark brace location lines on inside face of each rocker.

Centerline of brace

Ⓐ

Ⓒ

5/32" hole drilled to ¾" later for footrest

R = 2½"

5/32" hole

Stirrup opening

Brad locations

18"

18"

hole for the footrest (see the Rocker Grid drawing for locations). By drilling through both rockers, you've assured precise alignment of the ¾" footrest dowel later.

7 Sand the edges of the rockers to remove the saw marks (we belt-sanded the rocker bottoms and drum-sanded the harder-to-get-at areas around the stops). Wrap sandpaper around a strip of thin stock, and use it to sand the edges of the stirrup openings. Separate the two rockers, remove the grid paper, and sand smooth.

8 To make a jig for drilling the angled footrest holes through each rocker, start by ripping a 12" length of 2 × 4 in half. Set one of the pieces aside, and drill a ¾" hole 3½" deep centered into either end of the other piece. Miter-cut the scrap at 15° so that the saw cut intersects the ¾" hole. Then, draw a centerline along the longest face of the jig.

9 Use a framing square to mark a line centered through the 5/32" pilot hole perpendicular with the beveled-top edge of each rocker. Clamp the jig in place parallel with the beveled top edge of the rocker and centered on the line drawn through the 5/32" hole as shown in the photo *above right*. Drill the ¾"

dowel hole through the rocker. Repeat with the other rocker.

10 Using a ¼" round-over bit, rout both edges of the stirrup opening in each rocker. Readjust the ¼" round-over bit to leave a 3/32" shoulder. Rout the edges of each rocker to form a bead (see the Bead Detail that accompanies the Exploded View drawing.) Don't rout the top beveled edge of either rocker. Round off the end of the bead (where it meets the top beveled edge) with a chisel, then sand it to finished shape.

Build and assemble the body

1 First, cut the seat (B) oversize, then bevel-rip both edges at 15° to a 4⅜" width. Bevel-cut both ends at the same angle to a 18¾" length.

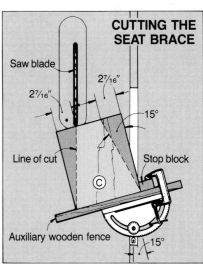

CUTTING THE SEAT BRACE

Saw blade

2⁷/₁₆"

2⁷/₁₆"

15°

Line of cut

Stop block

Ⓒ

Auxiliary wooden fence

15°

Mark the location of the six rocker mounting screw holes on the top of the seat. Drill ⅜" holes ¼" deep at these points. Switch to a 5/32" bit and drill the screw-shank holes centered in the ⅜" holes you just drilled (see the Screw Hole detail on the Exploded View drawing).

2 From ¾" stock, rip and crosscut a piece 7¾" wide by 9" long for the seat brace (C). Set your tablesaw miter gauge to 15° left of center, and attach an auxiliary wooden fence and stop where shown in the drawing *above*. Rip the seat brace, flip the brace over, and rip the other side.

Continued

Rocking Horse

3 Lay out the radii on the seat brace where shown in the Brace drawing on the opposite page. Cut the bottom edge of the seat brace to shape and drum-sand it.

4 Using the Rocker Grid drawing as a guide, mark the location of the brace (C) on the inside face of each of the rockers.

5 Clamp one of the rockers in a vise with its beveled top edge facing up. Position the seat on the rocker. Then, drill 7/64" pilot holes into the top edge of the rocker, using the 5/32" shank holes in the seat as a guide. (Be careful to keep the drill perpendicular to the seat to avoid drilling through the inside face of the rocker.) Now, glue and screw the seat to the rocker. Use the same procedure to attach the seat to the other rocker.

6 Remove the assembly from the vise. Slide the brace (C) into position between the rockers, centered between the lines drawn on the inside faces. Drill 7/64" pilot holes 3/4" deep into the brace centered in the 5/32" shank holes drilled earlier in the rockers. Glue and screw the rockers to the brace.

7 Plane a scrap of cherry 5/16" thick. Use a 3/8" plug cutter to cut plugs 5/16" long from the scrap. Glue the plugs over the screws, taking care to match the direction of the grain. Sand the plugs flush.

Topping things off

1 Rip and crosscut two pieces of 3/4" cherry to 9×10" for the head (D). Glue and clamp the pieces together face-to-face. When dry, trim the bottom for a square edge.

2 With a ruler and a straightedge, lay out 1" squares to form a 10×11" grid pattern on a piece of paper. Using the Head Grid drawing as a guide, transfer the shape of the head (as well as the eye and rein locations) to the grid paper. Attach the pattern to your stock with spray adhesive. Cut the head to shape, and sand the edges.

3 With a 1/4" bit, drill the eye holes 1/8" deep. Switch to a 3/4" bit, and drill the rein hole, backing the head with scrap to prevent chipout. Remove the grid paper and sand off any sticky residue.

4 Cut the saddle pieces (E, F) to finished size, bevel-cutting one end of each piece at 15°. Mark the radii where indicated in the Exploded View drawing, and cut the pieces to shape. Sand the radiused edges.

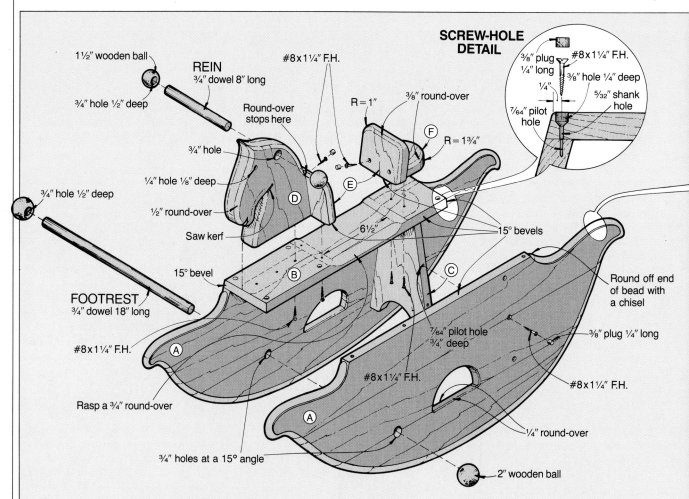

Using a table-mounted router with a ⅜″ round-over bit, rout the top and side edges of the saddle pieces that will face the rider. (To make sure we routed the correct edges, we first held the pieces in place on the body and marked the edges to be routed.)

5 Dry-clamp the front saddle piece to the horse's head, with the bottom edges flush. Make a mark on the head where the top edge of the saddle intersects it. Drill three mounting holes through the saddle piece and into the head to the sizes shown in the Screw Hole detail. Separate the pieces and rout the edges of the head using a ½″ round-over bit where shown in the Exploded View drawing. Use a chisel to complete the round-over where the jaw meets the neck.

6 Glue and screw the front saddle piece to the head, then dry-clamp the head assembly to the body. Using the same bit combination used earlier, drill and counterbore three screw holes through the seat and into the head. Glue and screw the head assembly in place.

7 Drill the mounting holes, then glue and screw the remaining saddle piece (E) to (F). Now, glue and screw this assembly to the seat leaving 6½″ between it and the front saddle piece.

8 Drill a ¾″ hole ½″ deep in each of the four wooden balls to accept the footrest and rein dowels. (To hold the balls steady while drilling, we bored a 1″ hole through a piece of ¾″ scrap. Then, we set each ball, end grain up, in the hole, and clamped it in a handscrew. Finally,

we clamped the assembly to our drill-press table as shown in the photo *below*.

9 Cut the ¾″ footrest and rein dowels to length (18″ and 8″ respectively). Then, insert the dowels to within ¾″ of their final centered position. Spread glue all the way around each dowel and push each dowel into position. Glue the 2″ wooden balls onto the ends of the footrest dowel and the 1½″ balls onto the ends of the rein.

10 Rasp a ¾″ round-over on the seat edges between the saddle pieces (E). Sand both of the round-overs smooth.

11 Finish-sand the entire horse, paying particular attention to the contours of the head. Apply several coats of finish, rubbing lightly with steel wool between coats.

Buying Guide

● **Wooden balls.** Two 1½″ birch balls (#1346) and two 2″ birch balls (#1348). For the current price, contact Meisel Hardware Spec., P.O. Box 70, Mound, MN, 55364-0070. Or call 800-441-9870 or 612/471-8550 to order.🌳

Project Design: Kim Downing
Photographs: Hopkins Associates;
    Craig Anderson

BEAD DETAIL

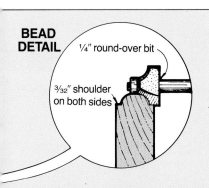

¼″ round-over bit

³⁄₃₂″ shoulder on both sides

BRACE

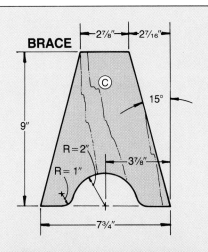

2⅞″ 2⁷⁄₁₆″

15°

9″

R = 2″

R = 1″

3⅞″

7¾″

HEAD GRID Each square = 1″

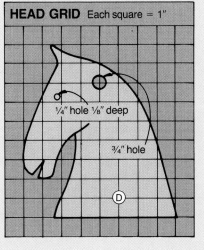

¼″ hole ⅛″ deep

¾″ hole

Bill of Materials

Part	Finished Size*			Material	Qty.
	T	W	L		
A*	¾″	11½″	36″	cherry (edge joined)	2
B*	¾″	4⅜″	18¾″	cherry	1
C*	¾″	7¾″	9″	cherry	1
D*	1½″	8″	9″	cherry (laminated)	1
E	¾″	4″	3¼″	cherry	2
F	¾″	3½″	3″	cherry	1

*Parts marked with an * are cut larger initially, then trimmed to finished size. Please read the instructions before cutting.

Supplies: double-faced tape, #8x1¼″ flathead wood screws, 1″ brads, paper for drawing grids, ¾″ birch dowel, spray adhesive, finish, #0000 steel wool

LONG-HAUL

Bill of Materials

Part	Finished Size			Material	Qty.
	T	W	L		
A	1½″	2″	2¼″	pine	1
B	¾″	1½″	4¾″	pine	1
C	1½″	3⅛″	11¾″	pine	1
D	¾″	1¾″ dia.		dark wood	6
E	½″	1¼″ dia.		dark wood	12
F	⅝″	1¼″ dia.		dark wood	1

Supplies: woodworker's glue, ¼″ and ⅜″ dowel stock, nontoxic finish.

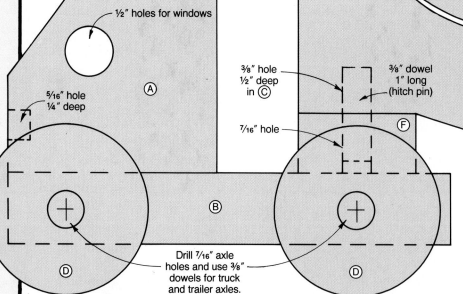

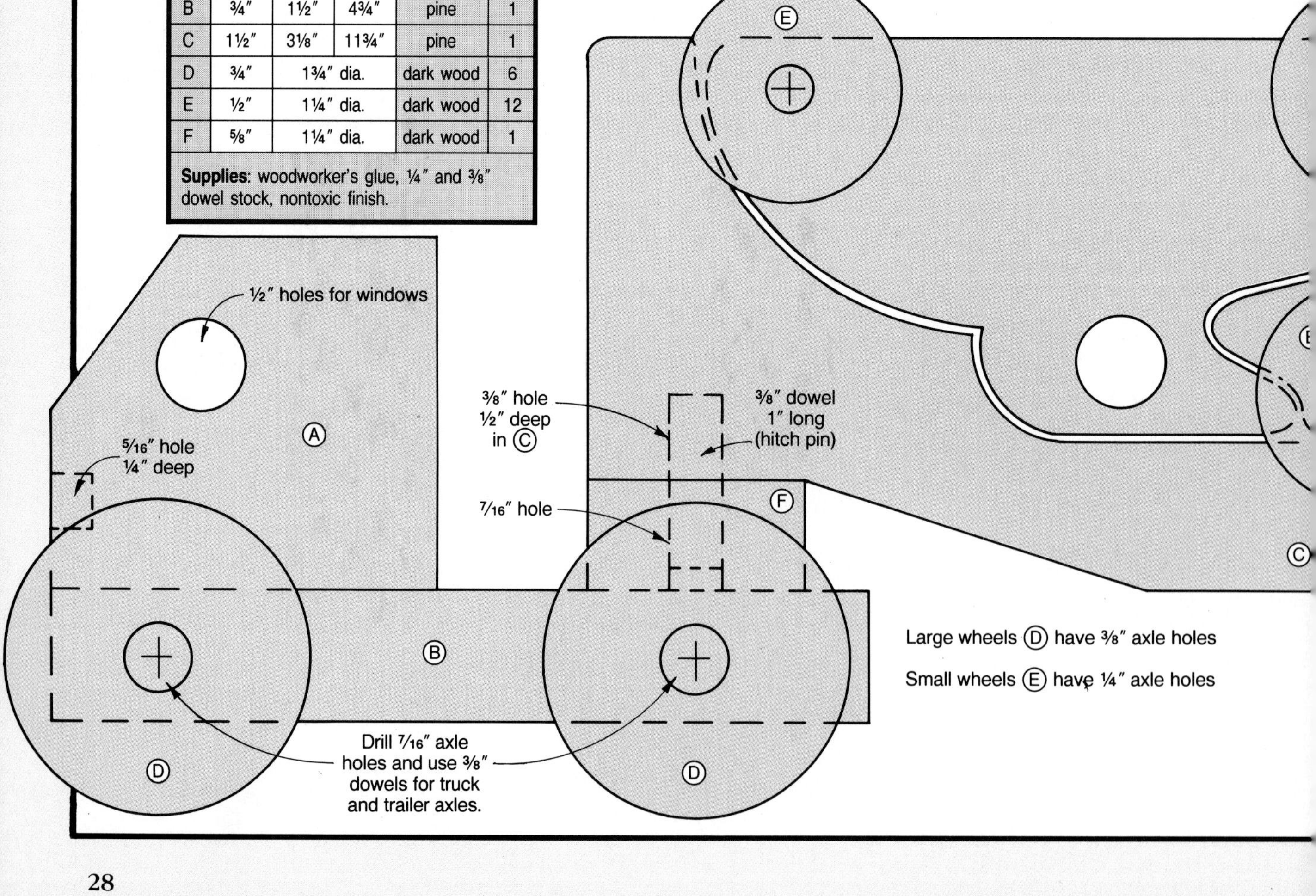

½″ holes for windows

Ⓐ

5/16″ hole ¼″ deep

⅜″ hole ½″ deep in Ⓒ

⅜″ dowel 1″ long (hitch pin)

7/16″ hole

Ⓔ

Ⓕ

Ⓒ

Ⓑ

Ⓓ

Ⓓ

Drill 7/16″ axle holes and use ⅜″ dowels for truck and trailer axles.

Large wheels Ⓓ have ⅜″ axle holes

Small wheels Ⓔ have ¼″ axle holes

TRANSPORT

Over-the-road tractor/trailer rigs fascinate most kids. This pint-size transport should prove equally intriguing, as your favorite youngster wheels it to all sorts of imaginary destinations.

1 Cut parts A, B, and C to the sizes listed in the Bill of Materials. Sand all the parts. Using a photocopy and spray adhesive or carbon paper, transfer the full-sized patterns to the stock. (Be sure to mark all the hole locations on the stock.)

2 Drill the 5/16″ axle holes and the 1/2″ window holes through the cars. Then, drill the 5/16″ headlight holes and 1/2″ window holes for the cab. Back up the stock with scrap wood to prevent chip-out.

3 Using a bandsaw or jigsaw, cut the cab to its final shape. Glue and clamp the cab to the base. After the glue dries, sand the cab, then drill the 7/16″ axle holes.

4 Cut out the trailer body and cars, using a bandsaw with a 1/8″ blade or a jigsaw. Cut the axle support out of the waste stock from the front of the trailer. Glue and clamp the support to the trailer, and then sand the trailer and all the cars.

5 Drill a 7/16″ axle hole for the trailer axle, and then drill the 3/8″ hole for the hitch pin.

6 Cut the truck, car, and fifth wheels (D, E, F) to size. The quickest way to make wheels is with a holesaw. Use a 2″ holesaw for the truck wheels (D) and a 1½″ holesaw for the car wheels (E) and the fifth wheel (F). Since holesaws have a 1/4″ pilot, you'll need to drill out the truck wheel holes to 3/8″ and the fifth wheel hole to 7/16″. Insert all axles, then glue all the wheels to the axles. Sand flush.

7 Finish this toy with two coats of a nontoxic finish such as salad bowl finish or mineral oil. ♣

Design: Steve Baldwin
Photograph: George Ceolla
Illustration: Mike Henry

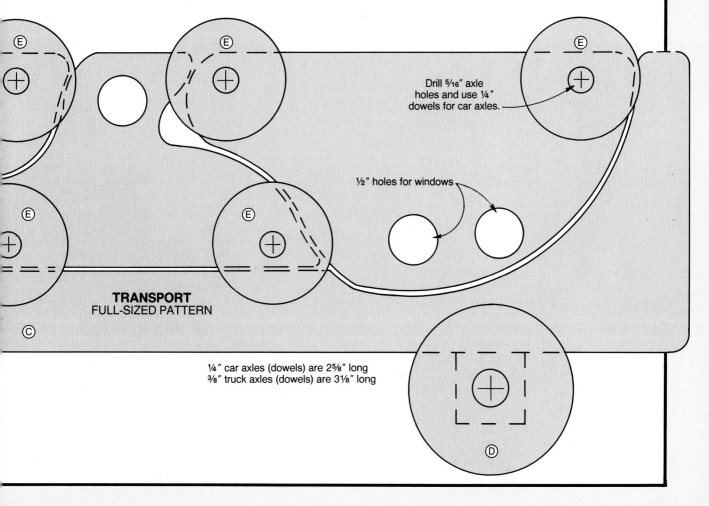

Drill 5/16″ axle holes and use 1/4″ dowels for car axles.

½″ holes for windows

TRANSPORT
FULL-SIZED PATTERN

¼″ car axles (dowels) are 2⅝″ long
⅜″ truck axles (dowels) are 3⅛″ long

THE "BIG APPLE" BANK

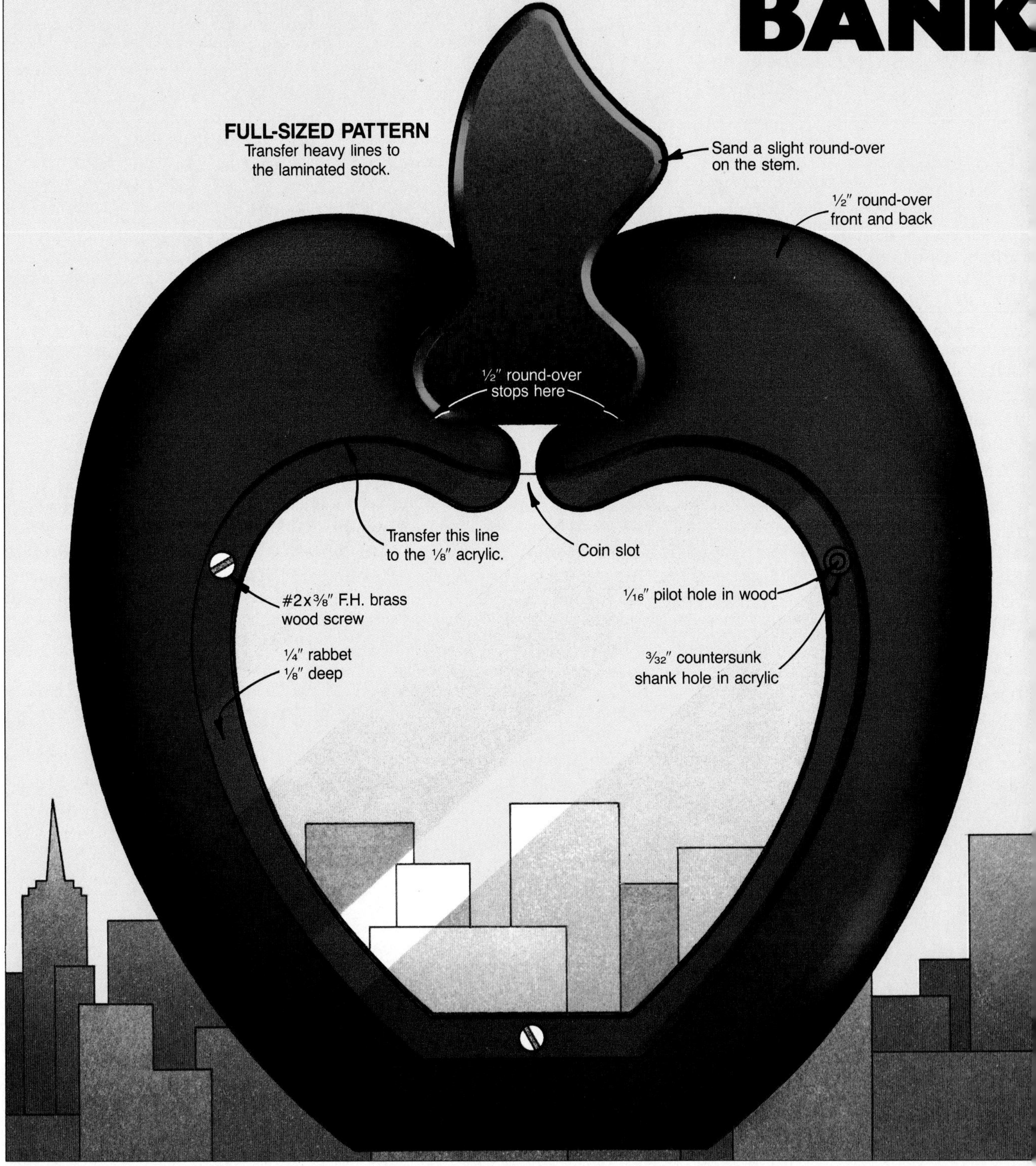

FULL-SIZED PATTERN
Transfer heavy lines to
the laminated stock.

Sand a slight round-over
on the stem.

½" round-over
front and back

½" round-over
stops here

Transfer this line
to the ⅛" acrylic.

Coin slot

#2x⅜" F.H. brass
wood screw

1/16" pilot hole in wood

¼" rabbet
⅛" deep

3/32" countersunk
shank hole in acrylic

What better way to teach your youngsters thrifty habits than with their very own apple savings bank, where they can see the pennies piling up. You can build the bank with just a band saw and router, and you may not need to travel any further than your scrap box for the materials.

1 Cut two pieces of ¾″ stock to 7x8″ (we used clear birch). Glue and clamp the two pieces together face to face to make a 1½″-thick blank. Later, after the glue dries, remove the clamps. Crosscut or plane the bottom edge of the blank to obtain a perfectly flat base.
2 Using carbon paper, transfer the full-sized apple and stem patterns to the laminated stock (don't forget the outline of the apple cavity).
3 Fit your band saw with a ⅛″ blade, and cut the outside outline of the apple and stem to shape. Remove the stem and cut the apple cavity to shape. Sand the cut edges of both pieces smooth to remove all saw marks.
4 Rout a ¼″ rabbet ⅛″ deep along the inside edge of the apple where shown in the drawing. (If you use a different size rabbeting bit, keep the ⅛″ depth the same, and adjust the size of the acrylic to fit the rabbeted opening.) Repeat the rabbeting procedure on the other face of the apple.
5 Rout a ½″ round-over along the outside edges of the apple, stopping short of the coin slot where shown on the drawing. Sand a slight round-over along the edges of the stem, and finish-sand the pieces.

6 Again using carbon paper, transfer the full-sized acrylic pattern onto a piece of paper. Stick two pieces of 5x5″ acrylic together with double-faced tape. Spray adhesive on the back of the pattern, and then stick it to the acrylic. Cut the acrylic to shape using the band saw and ⅛″ blade. Now, separate the two pieces of acrylic. Test-fit each in the rabbet, and sand the edges of the acrylic if necessary for a good fit.
7 Position an acrylic piece in each rabbet. Now, drill and countersink three ³/₃₂″ shank holes through the acrylic and just into the wood. Switch to a ¹/₁₆″ bit and drill a ¼″-deep pilot hole in the center of each ³/₃₂″ hole.

8 Apply a coat of sanding sealer to the apple body and stem. Lightly hand-sand, and then paint the apple red and the stem green. To hold the pieces while painting, drill ¼″ holes in the bottom of each apple part and two in a piece of plywood scrap. Mount each apple piece on an 8″ length of ¼″ dowel stock; then spray with a coat of gloss enamel.

(We stuck the dowel "handles" in the holes in the plywood until the paint dried, and later applied a second coat.)
9 Fasten each acrylic panel in position in the ¼″ rabbet, on front and back, with three #2x⅜″ flathead brass wood screws. ♠

Project Design: Tom Lewis
Photograph: Hopkins Associates
Illustration: Greg Roberts

Oh what fun it is to ride our Snow-loving

Minnesotans don't hibernate during winter; they march right outdoors and celebrate it. And in the Land of 10,000 Lakes and a lot of snow, we found this classic sleigh that stands up to the abuses of winter—and kids. After eight years of "testing" by his three children, Keith Raivo is ready to share his proven design.

open sleigh

First, laminate the runners

1 From ¾" particleboard or plywood, construct a bending form like the one dimensioned on the Bending Form Drawing.

2 From straight-grained 1¹⁄₁₆"-thick oak, rip 12 strips (this includes two extra strips in case of breakage) ⅛" thick by 52" long for the runners (A). The pieces are cut long and trimmed to length later.

3 Cover the form with waxed paper to prevent the strips from sticking (see the photo at *right* for reference). Then, cut a 1 × 1" scrap clamp bar 29" long.

4 Spread glue on the mating surfaces of five runner strips. For joints that will stand up to the extremes of Mother Nature, use either slow-set epoxy or resorcinol glue. Place the 52"-long strips against the form and flush with the straight end of the form. Then, position the clamp bar on the outside edge of the strips. Starting at the end with the cutoff slot, clamp the strips to the form, keeping the edges flush as shown in the photo at *right*. Let the lamination sit overnight.

5 Cut the tail end of the laminated runner to length with a backsaw, using the cut-off slot in the bending form. Remove the clamps and clamp bar. Repeat the process to make a second runner.

6 Scrape the squeeze-out from the edges of each runner and then sand the edges smooth. Cut the runner caps (B) to the size stated in the Bill of Materials. Glue and clamp one of them to each laminated runner, with the edges and tail ends flush. Later, cut or sand a slight curve on the top front edge of the runner cap where shown on the Runner Detail accompanying the Side Assembly Drawing. Rout ³⁄₁₆" round-overs along the edges of each runner.

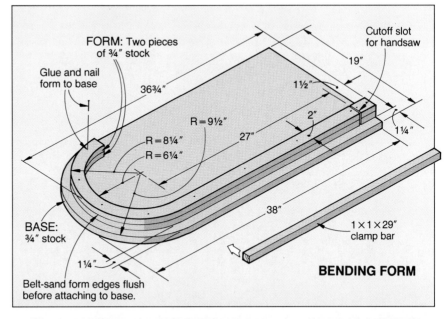

FORM: Two pieces of ¾" stock

Glue and nail form to base

Cutoff slot for handsaw

36¾"

19"

1½"

2"

R = 9½"

R = 8¼"

R = 6¼"

27"

1¼"

38"

BASE: ¾" stock

1 × 1 × 29" clamp bar

1¼"

Belt-sand form edges flush before attaching to base.

BENDING FORM

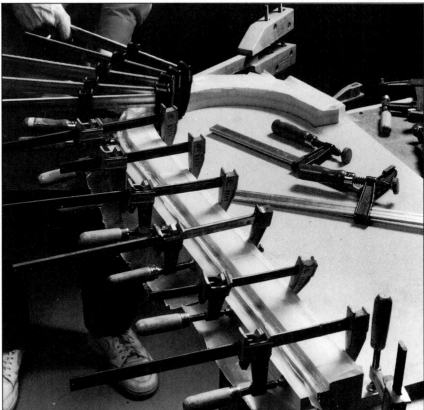

Starting at the straight end, clamp five ⅛"-thick oak strips to the bending form to laminate the runner.

Continued

Sleigh

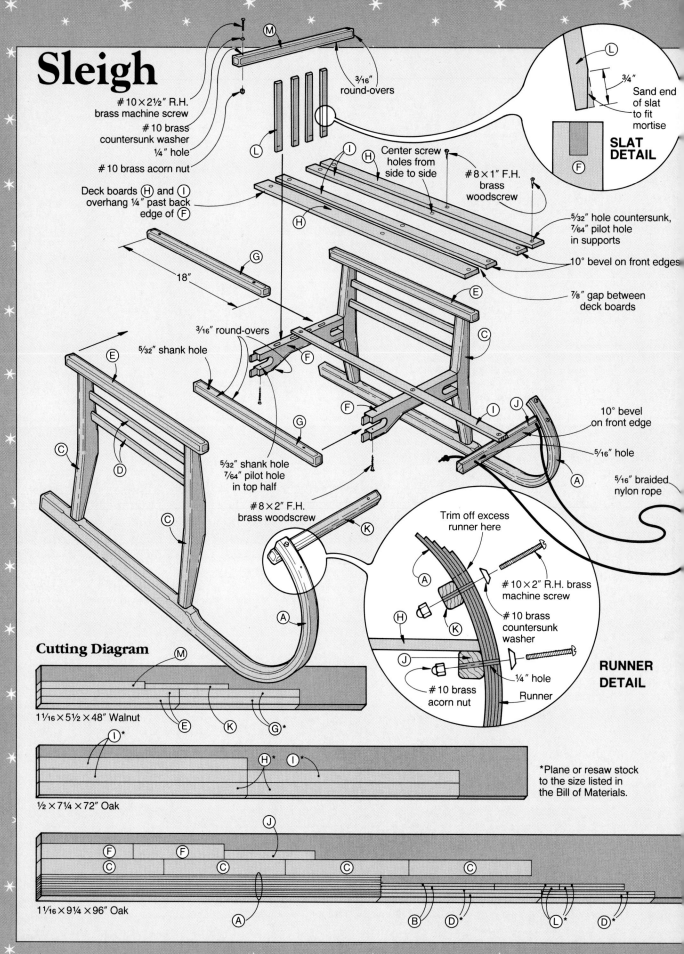

#10 × 2½″ R.H. brass machine screw

#10 brass countersunk washer

¼″ hole

#10 brass acorn nut

Deck boards Ⓗ and Ⓘ overhang ¼″ past back edge of Ⓕ

³⁄₁₆″ round-overs

Center screw holes from side to side

#8 × 1″ F.H. brass woodscrew

⁵⁄₃₂″ hole countersunk, ⁷⁄₆₄″ pilot hole in supports

10° bevel on front edges

⅞″ gap between deck boards

18″

³⁄₁₆″ round-overs

⁵⁄₃₂″ shank hole

⁵⁄₃₂″ shank hole ⁷⁄₆₄″ pilot hole in top half

#8 × 2″ F.H. brass woodscrew

10° bevel on front edge

⁵⁄₁₆″ hole

⁵⁄₁₆″ braided nylon rope

SLAT DETAIL

¾″

Sand end of slat to fit mortise

RUNNER DETAIL

Trim off excess runner here

#10 × 2″ R.H. brass machine screw

#10 brass countersunk washer

¼″ hole

#10 brass acorn nut

Runner

Cutting Diagram

1¹⁄₁₆ × 5½ × 48″ Walnut

½ × 7¼ × 72″ Oak

*Plane or resaw stock to the size listed in the Bill of Materials.

1¹⁄₁₆ × 9¼ × 96″ Oak

34

Bill of Materials

Parts		Finished Size*			Matl.	Qty.
		T	W	L		
A*	runners	5/8"	1 1/16"	48"	LO	2
B	runner caps	1/2"	1 1/16"	23 1/2"	O	2
C	uprights	1 1/16"	2 1/8"	18"	O	4
D	side slats	3/8"	3/4"	16 3/8"	O	4
E	rails	1 1/16"	1 1/16"	20"	W	2
F	slat supports	1 1/16"	2 1/2"	13 1/2"	O	2
G	rails	1"	1"	18"	W	2
H	deck boards	3/8"	2"	31 3/4"	O	2
I	deck boards	3/8"	1 1/2"	31 3/4"	O	3
J	support	1 1/16"	1 1/16"	13 1/2"	O	1
K	support	3/4"	1 1/16"	12 1/2"	W	1
L	backrest slats	3/8"	3/4"	9 1/4"	O	4
M	backrest rail	1 1/16"	1 1/16"	15 1/2"	W	1

*Initially cut parts marked with an * oversized. Then, trim each to finished size according to the how-to instructions.

Material Key: LO-laminated oak, O-oak, W-walnut

Supplies: waxed paper, #8×1" flathead brass wood screws, #8×2" flathead brass wood screws, #10×2" roundhead brass machine screws, #10×2 1/2" roundhead brass machine screws, #10 brass countersunk washers, #10 brass acorn nuts, clear exterior finish, 5/16" braided nylon rope 6' long.

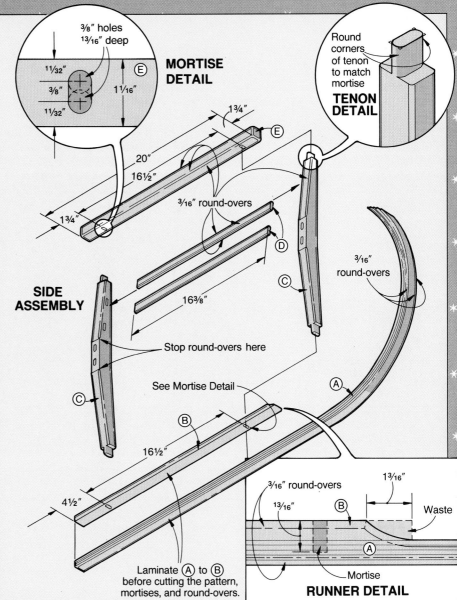

MORTISE DETAIL

3/8" holes 13/16" deep
11/32"
3/8"
11/32"
1 1/16"

TENON DETAIL
Round corners of tenon to match mortise

SIDE ASSEMBLY

1 3/4"
20"
16 1/2"
1 3/4"
3/16" round-overs
16 3/8"
3/16" round-overs
Stop round-overs here
See Mortise Detail
16 1/2"
4 1/2"
Laminate A to B before cutting the pattern, mortises, and round-overs.

RUNNER DETAIL
3/16" round-overs
13/16"
1 3/16"
13/16"
Waste
Mortise

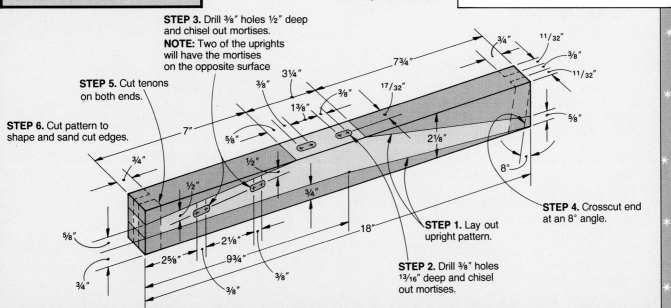

STEP 3. Drill 3/8" holes 1/2" deep and chisel out mortises.
NOTE: Two of the uprights will have the mortises on the opposite surface

STEP 5. Cut tenons on both ends.

STEP 6. Cut pattern to shape and sand cut edges.

STEP 1. Lay out upright pattern.

STEP 2. Drill 3/8" holes 13/16" deep and chisel out mortises.

STEP 4. Crosscut end at an 8° angle.

3/4"
11/32"
3/8"
11/32"
7 3/4"
17/32"
3 1/4"
3/8"
1 3/8"
2 1/8"
5/8"
8°
7"
5/8"
3/4"
1/2"
1/2"
3/4"
5/8"
2 1/8"
9 3/4"
2 5/8"
18"
3/4"
3/8"
3/8"

Sleigh

7 Mark the mortise locations on each runner where shown on the Side Assembly Drawing and accompanying Mortise Detail on the previous page. Drill ⅜″ holes ¹³/₁₆″ deep where marked. (After marking the mortise locations, we set the depth stop on our drill press to ensure a consistent depth from hole to hole. We also found it helpful to clamp the runners to the drill press-table when drilling the holes.) Remove the waste stock with a sharp chisel to finish forming each mortise.

Construct the side assemblies next

1 Cut four pieces of 1¹⁄₁₆″ oak stock to 2⅛″ wide by 18″ long for the uprights. Now, follow the six-step procedure on the Upright Drawing on the previous page to form the four uprights (C). As noted in Step 3 of the drawing, *make the uprights in pairs.* To do this, mark the ½″-deep mortises on opposite surfaces of two uprights—when the uprights are in the position shown on the Exploded-View Drawing, the mortises need to face each other.

2 With a file and sandpaper, round the square edges of the upright tenons where shown on the Tenon Detail accompanying the Side Assembly Drawing.

3 Cut the side slats (D) to size. Rout ³⁄₁₆″ round-overs along all four edges of each slat. Then, rout the same-sized round-overs along the edges of the uprights where shown on the Side Assembly Drawing. Check the fit of the slats into the mortises in the uprights.

4 Cut the walnut top rails (E) to size. Rout ³⁄₁₆″ round-overs along the edges and ends of each rail. Form the mortises on the bottom edge of each where dimensioned on the Side Assembly Drawing.

5 Dry-clamp the side-assembly pieces to check the fit. Trim if necessary. Glue and clamp together each side assembly, checking for square.

Now, shape the supports, and assemble the sleigh

1 Cut two pieces of 1¹⁄₁₆″ oak to 2½″ wide by 13½″ long for the slat supports (F). Using the Slat Support Drawing for reference, mark the slat-support outline and mortise locations on each piece.

2 Form the mortises. (To do this, we clamped a fence to our drill press and then drilled overlapping holes where marked.)

3 Cut rabbets across the ends of each slat support to form the tenons. Then, bandsaw the two supports to shape. Drum-sand the pieces to remove the saw marks.

4 Cut the lower walnut rails (G) to size. Rout ³⁄₁₆″ round-overs along the edges and ends of each lower rail.

5 Glue and clamp the slat supports between the two side assemblies, checking for square. Slide the lower rails into the notches in the slat supports and clamp them in place. The front edge of each rail should sit ¼″ in front of the front face of the front support. To secure the walnut rails (you'll want to work from the bottom side), drill the holes and drive the screws in place (see the Exploded-View Drawing for reference).

SLAT SUPPORT

It's time to add the deck boards

1 Cut the deck boards (H, I) to size, beveling the front ends at 10°. Cut the front deck-board support (J) to size, bevel-ripping the front edge at 10° where shown on the Exploded-View Drawing.

2 Rout or sand a ⅛″ round-over along the edges (but not the ends) of each deck board. Switch bits, and rout ³⁄₁₆″ round-overs on the deck-board support (J).

3 Locate and mark the center of each deck-board support. Then, drill the holes and fasten the deck boards to the deck-board supports, starting with the center deck board and working outward. See the Exploded-View Drawing for reference. From outside edge to outside edge, the total width of the deck should equal 12″.

4 Position the assembly on the sleigh. Then, mark the location and fasten the deck boards to the supports (F).

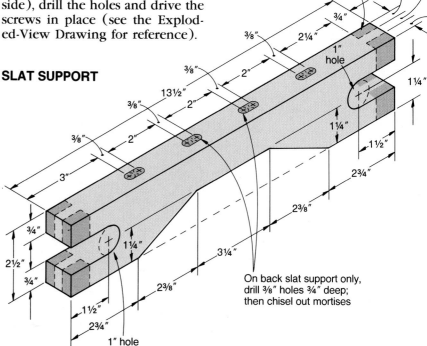

⅜″ tenon ¾″ long on both ends

On back slat support only, drill ⅜″ holes ¾″ deep; then chisel out mortises

5 Clamp a 2×4 to an outside deck board where shown in the photo *below*. (The 2×4 keeps the deck board straight.) Using the Runner Detail accompanying the Exploded-View Drawing for reference, drill the holes and screw the runner to the deck-board support (J). (To prevent the acorn nuts from working loose over time, we put a drop of epoxy in each nut before mating it with the machine screw.) Move the 2×4 to the other outside deck board and repeat the process.

6 Cut the top support (K) to size. Drill the holes and fasten it to the runners where shown on the Runner Detail.

7 With a fine-toothed saw, trim the top of each runner flush with the top of the runner support.

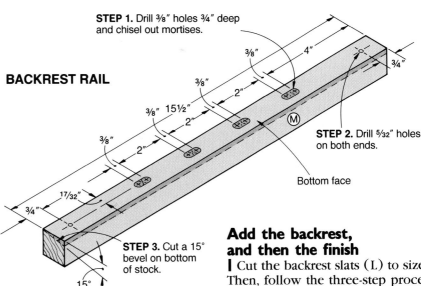

BACKREST RAIL

STEP 1. Drill ⅜" holes ¾" deep and chisel out mortises.

⅜" 4" ¾"

⅜" 2"

⅜" 15½"

⅜" 2"

M

STEP 2. Drill ⁵⁄₃₂" holes on both ends.

⅜" 2"

Bottom face

17/32"

¾"

STEP 3. Cut a 15° bevel on bottom of stock.

15°

Mark the centerpoint and drill a hole for fastening the deck-board support to the laminated runner. The 2×4 helps keep the deck boards flat.

Add the backrest, and then the finish

1 Cut the backrest slats (L) to size. Then, follow the three-step procedure on the Backrest Rail Drawing to cut the backrest rail (M) and locate and form its mortises.

2 Sand the bottom front end of the slats to fit into the mortises in the rear support (F). See the Slat Detail accompanying the Exploded-View Drawing for reference.

3 Glue the backrest slats into the mortises in the rear support (F). Now, fit the backrest rail (M) onto the top of the slats. Drill the holes and fasten the backrest rail to the top ends of the top rails.

4 Drill a pair of ⁵⁄₁₆" holes in the deck-board support (J) where shown on the Exploded-View Drawing to accept the pull rope.

5 Sand the sleigh. Apply the finish (we used three coats of clear exterior polyurethane, steel-wooling between coats). Add the braided nylon rope. Apply paraffin or ski wax to the bottom of the runners for added ease in sliding.

Buying Guide

● **Slow-set epoxy.** One pint can of resin, one pint of hardener, and instructions. For the current price, contact Smith & Co., 5100 Channel Ave., Richmond, CA 94804. Call 800-234-0330. ●

Project Design: Keith Raivo Designs,
 Brook Park Minnesota
Photographs: John Hetherington;
 Hopkins Associates
Illustrations: Kim Downing; Mike Henry

THEY DON'T BUILD 'EM LIKE THIS ANYMORE
DOLL CRADLE

Thank goodness for a photographer's attentive eye! William Hopkins, Sr., who shot many of the photos for this book, spotted this antique doll cradle while on assignment. And fortunately for us, Bill decided to jot down the dimensions and build one for a gift for a friend's daughter. When we saw Bill's handiwork, we fell for the project immediately. We think you will, too.

Edge-join stock to form the wide panels

Note: The cradle sides (A), back (B), front (C), base (D), and hood parts (E, F) require wide panels. When you edge-join boards to form these panels, we recommend using 4" or narrower boards to reduce the chance of warpage.

1 Glue and clamp enough ¾" cherry to form the following: two panels measuring 12×27⅝" for the cradle sides (A). A 9⅜×12½" panel for the cradle back (B), an 8×12" panel for the cradle front (C), a 12×25" panel for the cradle base (D), and two 6¼×12" panels for the hood parts (E, F).

After the glue dries, remove the clamps and sand each panel.
2 Resaw the two 6¼×12" panels for the hood parts (E, F) so you end up with four ¼"-thick panels. Sand each resawed panel smooth.
3 Cut the hood support blank (G) to 2½×13½". And cut two rocker blanks (H) to 3×18".

The compound angles: Easier than you think

1 Make a mark on the inside face of the front, back, and side panels as well as the hood support blank.
2 As shown on Step 1 of the three-step drawing *below*, tilt your tablesaw blade 10° right of vertical. Next, *with the marked inside face down,* cut a 10° bevel along the *bottom edge* of the sides (A), back (B), and front (C).
3 Using the dimensions on the Cradle Side, Back, Front, and Hood Support drawings, mark the angled cutlines on the *inside* face of these pieces. When making the cuts shown on Steps 2 and 3, save the cutoff end pieces from parts B and C; you'll use them later as clamp blocks when assembling the cradle.
4 Tilt your blade 3° right of vertical, and angle your miter gauge 10° from square where shown on Step 2 *below. With the inside face up,* cut the compound angle

where shown along the right-hand side of pieces A, B, C, and G.
5 With the inside face of each piece *up,* follow Step 3 to cut the compound angle along the opposite end of each piece.

Now, mark and cut all the pieces to shape

1 Using the dimensions on the Cradle Side Drawing and accompanying Grid Pattern, mark the layout for the top edge of one side panel. To enlarge the grid pattern for the curved portion of the sides, cut a piece of heavy paper to 3×6", and draw a 1" grid on the paper. Using the Grid Pattern as reference, lay out the curved outline on the marked grid. To do this, mark the points where the pattern outline crosses each grid line. Finally, draw lines to connect the points. Cut the paper pattern to shape, and use it as a template to mark the curved portion on each cradle side.
2 Bandsaw the top edge of the cradle side panel to shape. Trace its outline onto the other cradle side, and cut its top edge to shape.
3 Repeat the process in Step 1 *above* to mark the contoured-top shape of the cradle back (B), front (C), hood support (G), and rockers (H). Cut the pieces to shape and sand smooth.

Continued

STEP 1

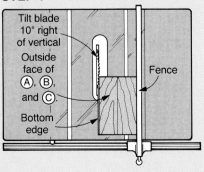

Tilt blade 10° right of vertical
Outside face of Ⓐ, Ⓑ, and Ⓒ
Bottom edge
Fence

STEP 2

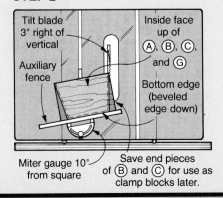

Tilt blade 3° right of vertical
Auxiliary fence
Inside face up of Ⓐ, Ⓑ, Ⓒ, and Ⓖ
Bottom edge (beveled edge down)
Miter gauge 10° from square
Save end pieces of Ⓑ and Ⓒ for use as clamp blocks later.

STEP 3

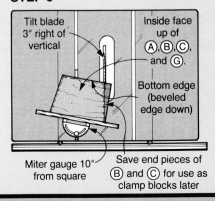

Tilt blade 3° right of vertical
Inside face up of Ⓐ, Ⓑ, Ⓒ, and Ⓖ.
Bottom edge (beveled edge down)
Miter gauge 10° from square
Save end pieces of Ⓑ and Ⓒ for use as clamp blocks later

DOLL CRADLE

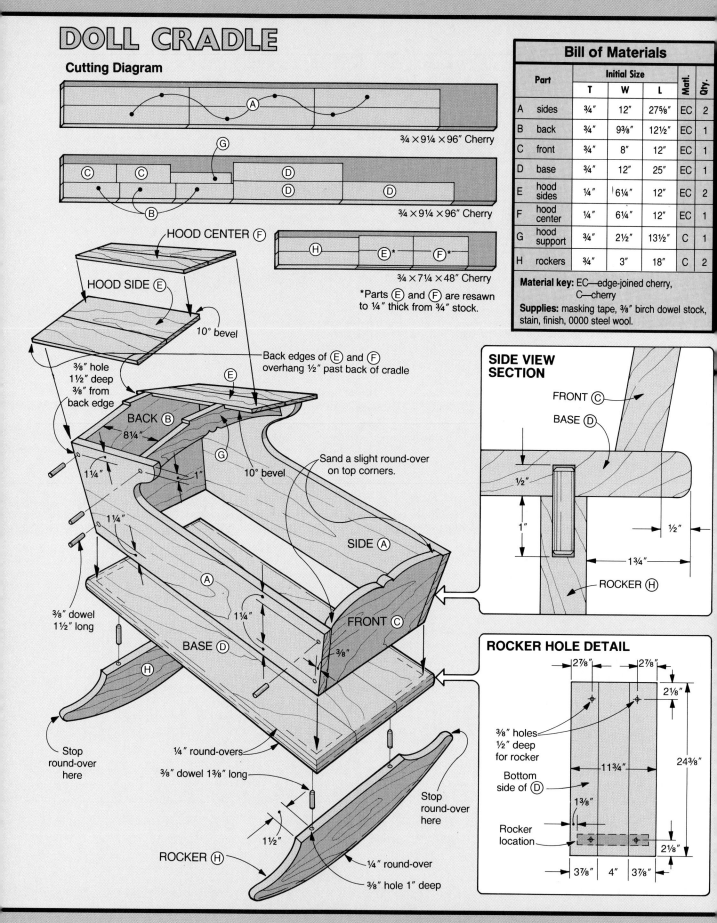

Cutting Diagram

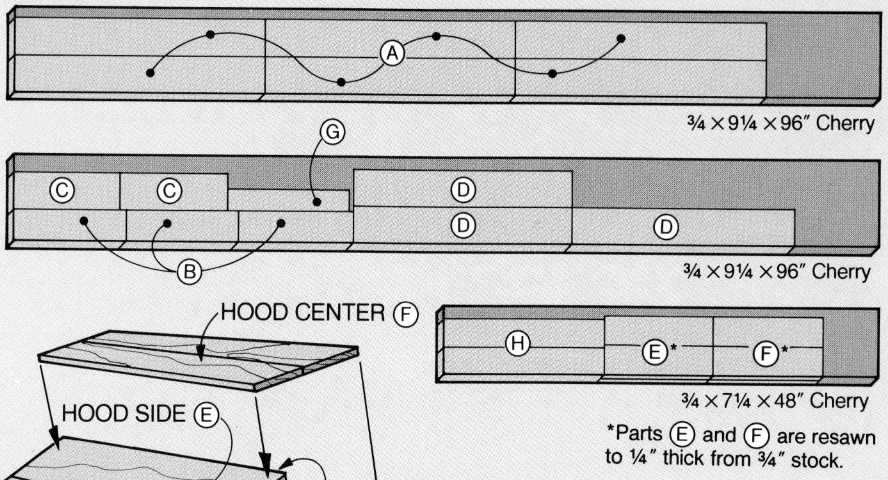

A
¾ × 9¼ × 96″ Cherry
G
C
C
D
D
D
B
¾ × 9¼ × 96″ Cherry
H
E*
F*
¾ × 7¼ × 48″ Cherry
*Parts E and F are resawn to ¼″ thick from ¾″ stock.

Part		Initial Size			Matl.	Qty.
		T	W	L		
A	sides	¾″	12″	27⅝″	EC	2
B	back	¾″	9⅜″	12½″	EC	1
C	front	¾″	8″	12″	EC	1
D	base	¾″	12″	25″	EC	1
E	hood sides	¼″	6¼″	12″	EC	2
F	hood center	¼″	6¼″	12″	EC	1
G	hood support	¾″	2½″	13½″	C	1
H	rockers	¾″	3″	18″	C	2

Bill of Materials

Material key: EC—edge-joined cherry, C—cherry

Supplies: masking tape, ⅜″ birch dowel stock, stain, finish, 0000 steel wool.

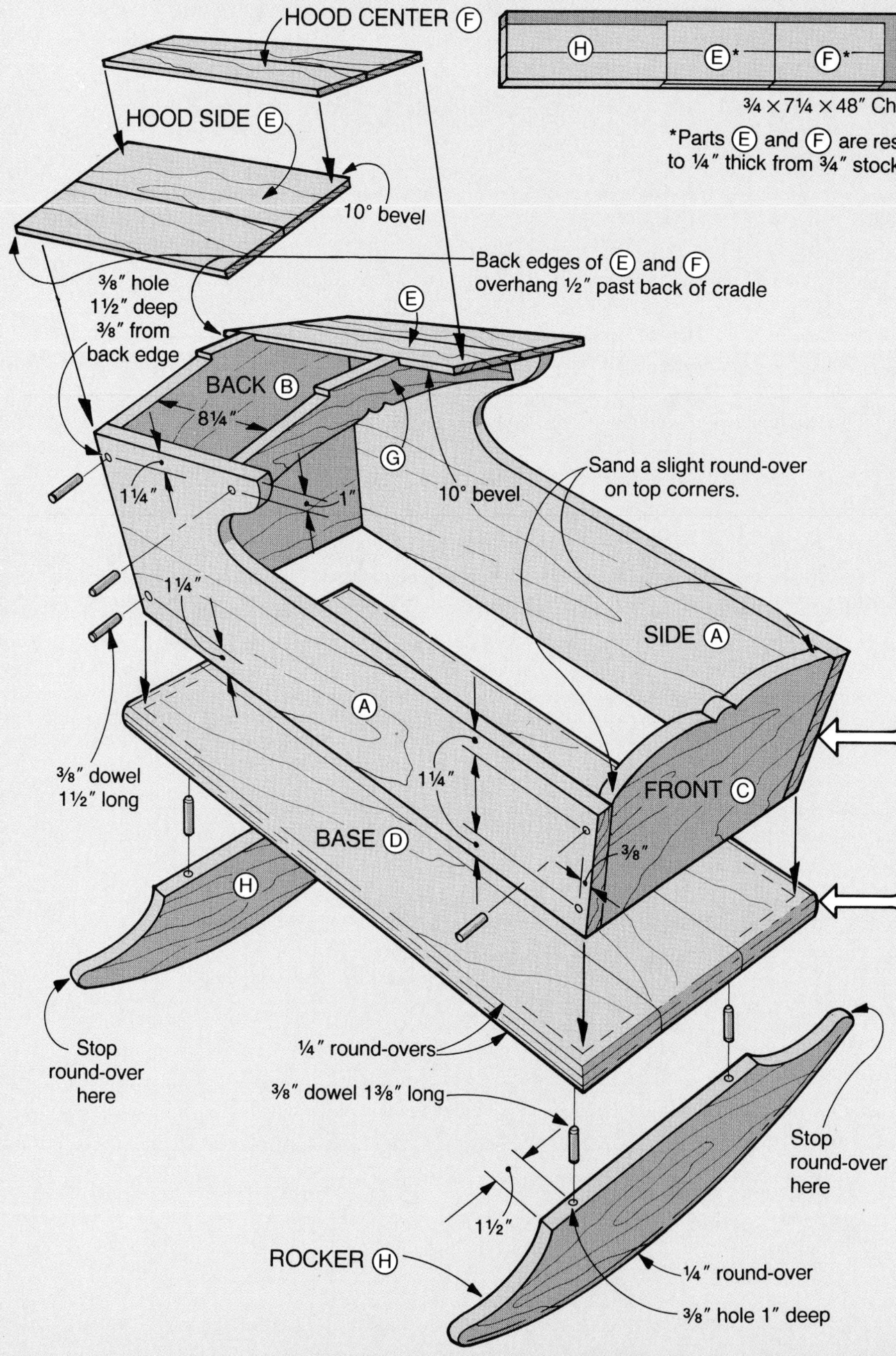

HOOD CENTER F
HOOD SIDE E
10° bevel
Back edges of E and F overhang ½″ past back of cradle
⅜″ hole 1½″ deep ⅜″ from back edge
E
BACK B
8¼″
G
10° bevel
Sand a slight round-over on top corners.
1¼″
1″
1¼″
SIDE A
A
1¼″
FRONT C
⅜″
BASE D
⅜″ dowel 1½″ long
H
Stop round-over here
¼″ round-overs
⅜″ dowel 1⅜″ long
Stop round-over here
1½″
ROCKER H
¼″ round-over
⅜″ hole 1″ deep

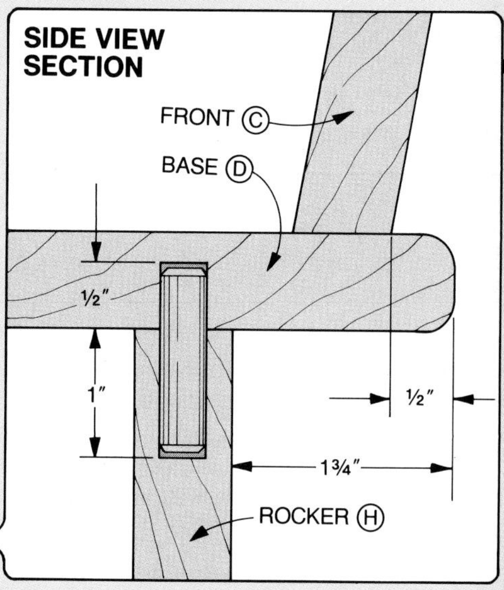

SIDE VIEW SECTION
FRONT C
BASE D
½″
1″
½″
1¾″
ROCKER H

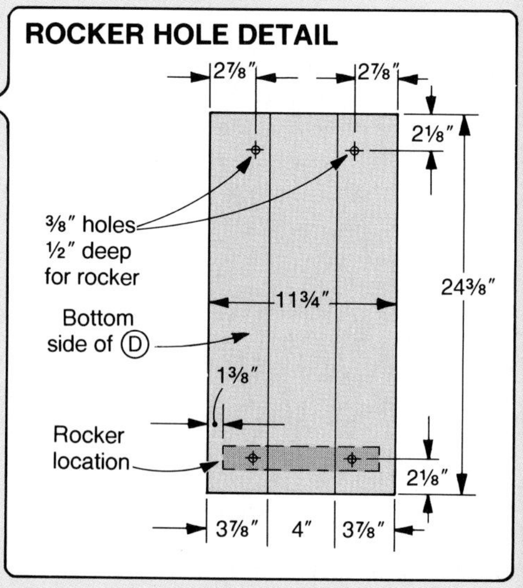

ROCKER HOLE DETAIL
2⅞″
2⅞″
2⅛″
⅜″ holes ½″ deep for rocker
11¾″
24⅜″
Bottom side of D
1⅜″
Rocker location
2⅛″
3⅞″
4″
3⅞″

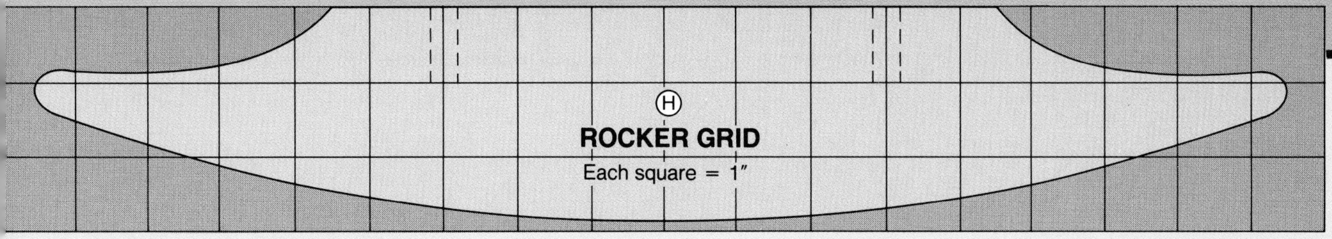
H
ROCKER GRID
Each square = 1″

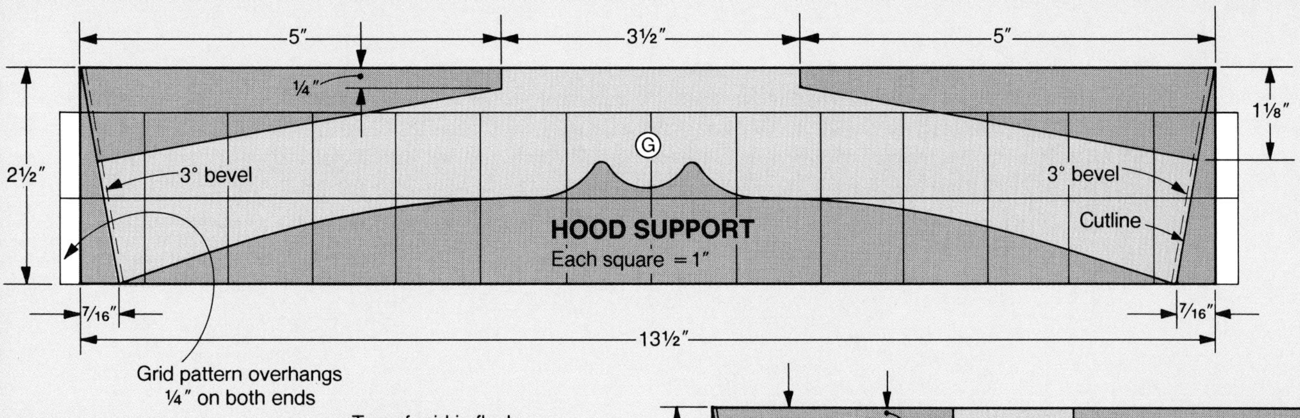
5″
3½″
5″
¼″
1⅛″
2½″
G
3° bevel
3° bevel
HOOD SUPPORT
Each square = 1″
Cutline
7/16″
7/16″
13½″
Grid pattern overhangs
¼″ on both ends

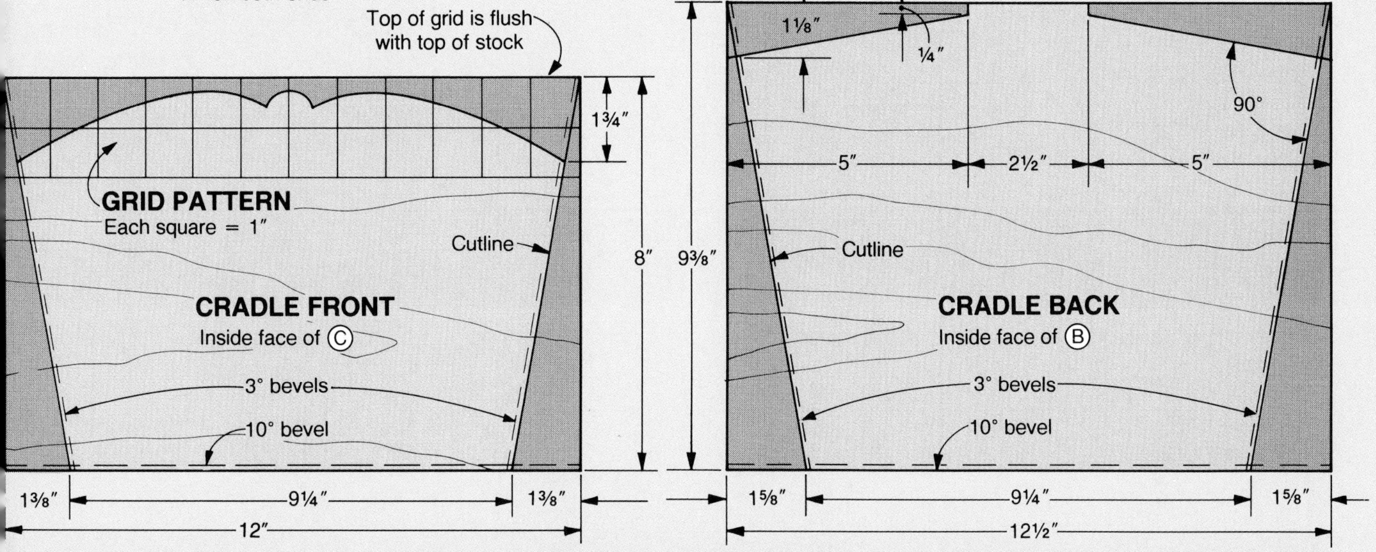
Top of grid is flush
with top of stock
1¾″
GRID PATTERN
Each square = 1″
Cutline
CRADLE FRONT
Inside face of C
3° bevels
10° bevel
8″
9⅜″
1⅜″
9¼″
1⅜″
12″
1⅛″
¼″
90°
5″
2½″
5″
Cutline
CRADLE BACK
Inside face of B
3° bevels
10° bevel
1⅝″
9¼″
1⅝″
12½″

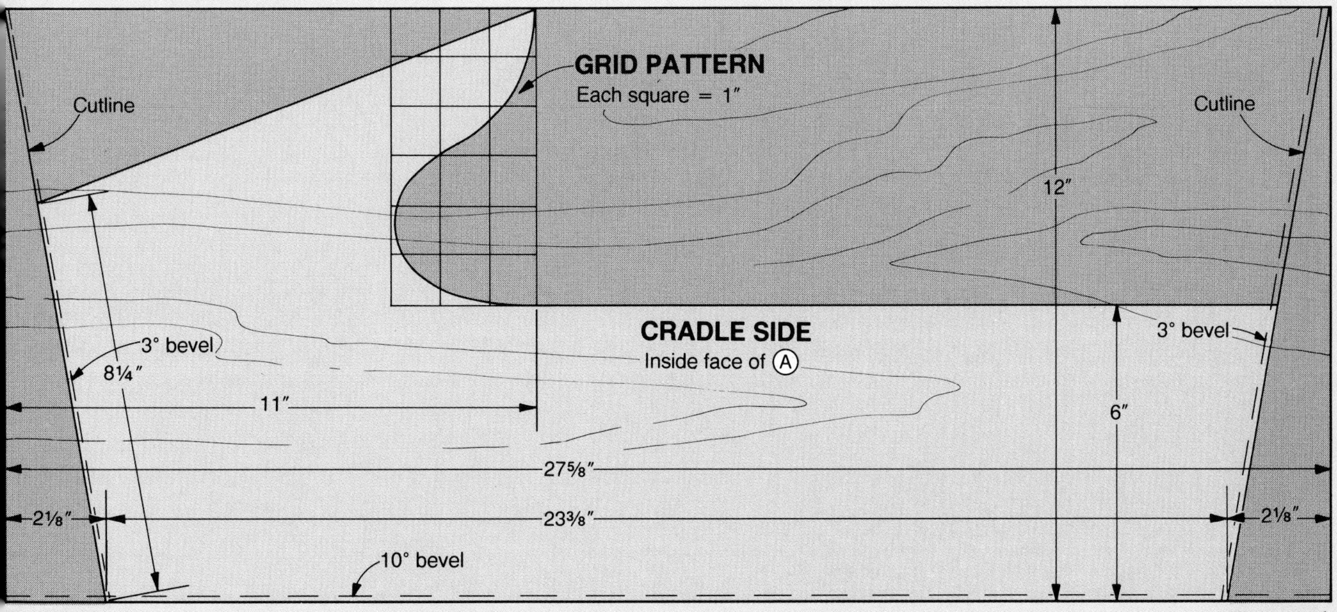
Cutline
GRID PATTERN
Each square = 1″
Cutline
12″
CRADLE SIDE
Inside face of A
3° bevel
3° bevel
8¼″
11″
6″
27⅝″
2⅛″
23⅜″
2⅛″
10° bevel

Continued

DOLL CRADLE

The cradle begins to take shape

1 Cut the cradle base (D) to size from the edge-joined cherry panel, and rout ¼″ round-overs along all edges. Rout ¼″ round-overs along the *bottom* edge of each rocker (see the Exploded View drawing for reference).

2 Using masking tape and a helper, dry-clamp the front, back, and hood support between the cradle sides to check the fit; trim if necessary. Mark a slight round-over on the top corner edges of the front (C) where they meet the side pieces. Remove the tape, and cut or sand the round-overs to shape. (Again, see the Exploded View drawing for reference.)

3 Apply glue to the mating areas (set the hood support aside for now). As shown in the photo *be-low*, clamp the assembly together, using the cutoff end pieces as clamping blocks. Make sure that the ends of the cradle side pieces are flush with the outside faces of the cradle front and back. Also check the cradle assembly for square. Immediately remove any excess glue with a damp cloth. After the glue dries, remove the clamps and sand smooth.

4 Now, glue the cherry hood support in place (we held ours in position with masking tape until the glue dried).

5 Using the dimensions on the Exploded View drawing, mark the dowel centerpoints on each side piece (each side has five holes). Now, as shown in the photo at *right*, drill ⅜″ holes 1½″ deep where marked (we used a brad-point bit).

6 From ⅜″ birch dowel, cut 10 dowels 1⁹⁄₁₆″ long. Sand a chamfer on one end of each. Glue the dowels in place, inserting the chamfered ends first. Sand the protruding ends of the dowels flush with the cradle surfaces.

7 Center the cradle assembly on the base. Lightly trace the cradle's outline onto the top surface of the

Using the cutoff scraps as clamp blocks, glue and clamp the cradle front and back between the side pieces.

Carefully mark the dowel hole center-points on each side panel. Then, using a

base. To prevent the joints from cracking later due to expansion and contraction, apply glue only to the bottom of the side pieces—do not glue the bottom edges of the front and back to the base. Using clamp blocks, clamp the assembly onto the base where marked. Immediately wipe off any excess glue with a damp cloth.

portable electric drill and a brad point bit, drill ⅜″ holes 1½″ deep.

"As we do with all our projects, we built this cradle in our shop to check the procedure, dimensions, and angles. In fact, we ended up building several cradles to ensure accuracy and provide you with the best instructions possible." *Marlen Kemmet* *How-To Editor*

Attach the rockers

1 Using the dimensions on the Rocker Hole detail accompanying the Exploded View drawing, mark and drill four ⅜″ holes ½″ deep in the bottom of the base.

2 Insert a pair of ⅜″ dowel centers in the holes in one end of the base. Hold a rocker in position on the bottom side of the base (see the Rocker Hole Detail for location). Squeeze the rocker against the base to transfer the hole centerpoints to the rocker. Repeat for the second rocker. Drill a pair of ⅜″ holes 1″ deep in each rocker where indented. (We used a doweling jig when drilling the holes.)

3 Cut four ⅜″ dowels to 1⅜″ in length. Sand a chamfer on both ends of each dowel.

4 Glue, dowel, and clamp the rockers to the bottom of the base.

The hood tops off the cradle assembly

1 Using the dimensions on the Hood Center Drawing, mark the outline and cut the hood center (F) to shape.

2 Bevel-rip the inside edge of each of the hood sides at 10°. (See Step 1 on the three-step drawing on page 39 for help with this if necessary.)

3 Glue and clamp the hood sides (E) to the top edge of the side pieces. To allow the hood sides to expand and contract without splitting, *do not* glue them to the back or the hood support. The back edge of the hood sides should overhang the back edge of the cradle by ½″. (We used masking tape to hold the pieces in place until the glue dried.)

4 Glue and clamp the hood center in place; it also over hangs the back edge by ½″.

Add the finish and the dolly

1 Finish-sand the entire cradle. Stain as desired. (We used a cherry stain. Since cherry darkens with age, we avoided dark stains.)

2 Apply the finish (we used polyurethane sanding sealer and three coats of semigloss polyurethane). Wrap a ribbon around the cradle and present it to a lucky child. 🌲

Photographs: Hopkins Associates; Bob Calmer
Illustrations: Kim Downing; Bill Zaun

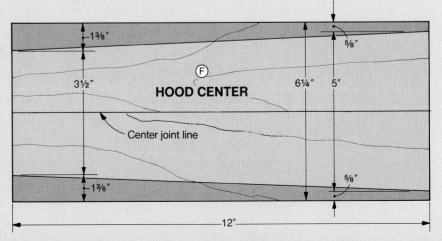

1⅜″

5⁄8″

3½″

Ⓕ

HOOD CENTER

6¼″ 5″

Center joint line

1⅜″

5⁄8″

12″

A NIFTY PROJECT WITH ONLY ONE STRING ATTACHED
SCRAPWOOD YO-YO

Dollar for dollar, it's hard to beat the enjoyment kids—or adults—get from playing with yo-yos. We think you'll have fun making them, too.

³⁄₈" dowel
⁵⁄₈" long

³⁄₈" hole
¼" deep

First, construct the jig

1 Mark a 3"-diameter circle and a 1½"-diameter circle on a piece of ¾"-thick scrap stock. Band-saw the discs to shape.
2 Glue and clamp the smaller disc to the center of the larger disc (locating it exactly on center isn't critical).
3 Fasten the 3" disc to a 3" faceplate and thread onto the headstock spindle. Slide the tailstock against the smaller disc to make a slight indention at the disc's center. Back the tailstock away, and drill a ³⁄₈" hole ³⁄₈" deep at the center point.
4 Glue a ³⁄₈" dowel ⁵⁄₈" long into the hole you just drilled.

Now, turn the yo-yo parts

1 Mark a pair of 2½"-diameter circles on a piece of highly figured scrap stock. Band-saw the discs to shape.
2 Drill a ³⁄₈" hole ¼" deep at the center point of each disc.
3 Using hot-melt adhesive, glue one of the yo-yo halves flat against the 1½"-diameter jig disc.
4 Turn the yo-yo half to a 2⅛" diameter, and then turn the piece to ½" thick. Next, turn a ³⁄₈" radius on the outside corners (we used a small

gouge). Check the radius with a ³⁄₈" round-over bit as shown in the photo *below*. Sand a slight round-over on the inside edge. Finsh-sand the yo-yo half. Using a 1" chisel and a mallet, gently tap between the yo-yo half and 1½"-diameter disc to separate the two parts. Pry at several different spots for an easy release.

Check the turned radius with a ³⁄₈" round-over bit.

5 Scrape the hot-melt adhesive off the jig, and sand the inside face of the yo-yo half. Repeat the procedure to turn the other half. Hold the two halves together and check the shapes. You want the two halves identical in profile and size for a true-spinning yo-yo. Remount and turn one half if necessary.
6 Cut a piece of ³⁄₈" dowel to ⁵⁄₈" long, and glue the two halves together. Apply the finish.
7 Order the yo-yo strings and trick book from the source listed in the Buying Guide.

Buying Guide
● **Strings and book.**
Ten yo-yo strings and a yo-yo book for $2 ppd. from Duncan Trick Book Offer, P.O. Box 5, Middlefield, OH 44062. 🌳

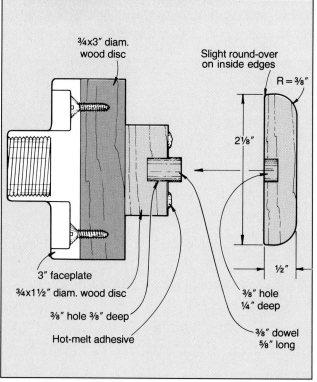

¾x3" diam. wood disc

Slight round-over on inside edges

R = ³⁄₈"

2⅛"

½"

3" faceplate
¾x1½" diam. wood disc
³⁄₈" hole ³⁄₈" deep
Hot-melt adhesive

³⁄₈" hole ¼" deep

³⁄₈" dowel ⁵⁄₈" long

Project Design: Marlen Kemmet   Photographs: Hopkins Associates   Illustrations: Kim Downing; Bill Zaun

FANCIFUL ZOO CAROUSEL

Oh my! We don't have any lions, and tigers, and bears. But we do offer a giraffe, zebra, rhino, and elephant to adorn our spinning zoo carousel. Wind the platform by hand and then watch it twirl around and rewind itself time and time again. Warning: This activity may be wonderfully habit-forming for children and adults.

Shape the carousel

1 Glue and clamp enough ¾"-thick maple together edge to edge to make a board at least 9×9" for the platform (A). Later, scrape off the excess glue, and trim to 9×9".

2 Draw diagonals from corner to corner to find the center of the maple square. Then, mark the four circles (radii measure 2¼", 2½", 3¼", and 4") where shown on the Platform drawing. Mark the small radii (¼", ¾") on the platform where dimensioned on the drawing. Mark the four screw eye centerpoints on the 2½" radius.

3 Use a bandsaw fitted with a ⅛" blade to cut the platform to shape.

Drum-sand the curves smooth.

4 Drill a ⁷⁄₁₆" hole in the center of the platform. Drill a ¹⁄₁₆" pilot hole ⅜" deep for each screw eye.

5 Mark a 4½"-diameter circle on a piece of ¾"-thick maple for the base (B). Cut it to shape.

6 Drill a ⅜" hole ½" deep into center of the base.

7 Cut a piece of ⅜" dowel 12" long. Use a bandsaw, cut two ¹⁄₁₆" saw kerfs ¼" deep, perpendicular to each other in the end of the dowel (see the Dowel detail).

8 Glue the unkerfed end of the dowel into the hole in the base. Use a square to check that the dowel is perpendicular to the base.

9 To make the knob (C), mark a 1"-diameter circle on a piece of ¾" thick maple. Drill a ⅜" hole ½" deep at the center of the marked circle. Now, cut the circle to shape. Sand a slight round-over along the top edge of the knob.

And now, the animals

1 Using carbon paper, transfer the full-sized animal patterns to ¾"-thick stock, noting the grain direction on the patterns. (We used walnut for the elephant and rhino, and zebrawood for the zebra and giraffe for contrast.)

2 Cut the animals to shape. Sand the bandsawed edges smooth.

Continued

Final assembly

1 Sand all parts of the project. Mix and place a dab of epoxy on the bottom of the feet of all the animals. Position the animals on the platform, and let the epoxy cure.

2 Apply self-adhesive rubber or cork feet (also called bumpers) to the bottom of the base to prevent the base from slipping when the platform is wound up. Apply finish.

3 Position two ¼″-thick spacers on the top of the base, and slide the platform down the dowel onto the spacers. Using heavy-duty thread, tie the thread to one screw eye. Pull the thread through a saw kerf in the top of the dowel, snug it up, and tie it to the opposite screw eye. As shown in the photo *below*, repeat for the second thread, keeping an equal tension on both threads.

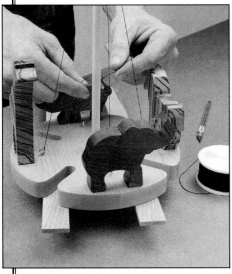

Support the platform on the base with scrap spacers. Hang the platform from the center dowel.

4 Remove the spacers, and add the knob to the top of the dowel. Rotate the platform several revolutions and let it twirl. After you're done playing with it, call the kids.

Supplies: 4-small screw eyes (we used Stanley 8450-212 1/2 eyes, ¹³⁄₁₆″ long with ³⁄₁₆″ inside eye diameter), heavy-duty thread or nylon fishing line, nonskid feet. 🌳

Project Design: William Warrick
Photographs: Bob Calmer, Jim Kascoutas
Illustrations: Kim Downing, Bill Zaun

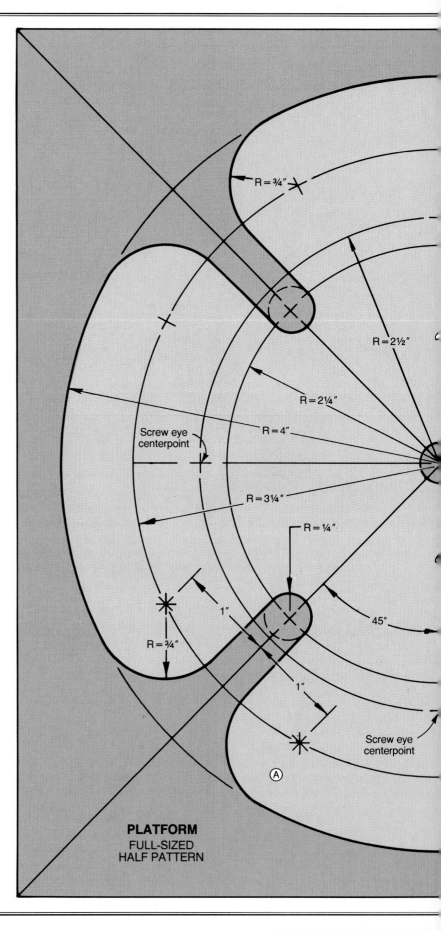

R = ¾″

R = 2½″

R = 2¼″

R = 4″

Screw eye centerpoint

R = 3¼″

R = ¼″

1″

45°

R = ¾″

1″

Screw eye centerpoint

Ⓐ

PLATFORM
FULL-SIZED
HALF PATTERN

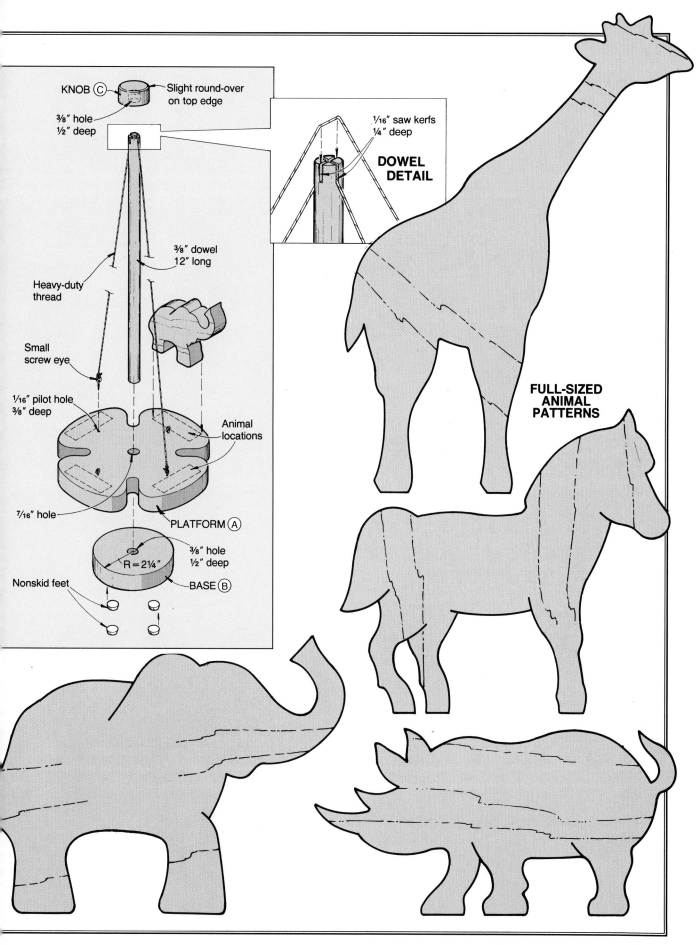

KNOB C

Slight round-over
on top edge

3/8" hole
1/2" deep

1/16" saw kerfs
1/4" deep

DOWEL
DETAIL

3/8" dowel
12" long

Heavy-duty
thread

Small
screw eye

1/16" pilot hole
3/8" deep

Animal
locations

7/16" hole

PLATFORM A

3/8" hole
1/2" deep

R = 2 1/4"

Nonskid feet

BASE B

FULL-SIZED
ANIMAL
PATTERNS

HEAVY HAULIN

Note: The instructions and the parts listed in the Bill of Materials are for one tractor. Cut twice as many parts if you want to build two tractors.

Start with the tractor

1 Cut a piece of ¾" pine to 2" wide by 12" long for the cab parts (A).

2 Measuring 1" from each end of the pine, mark the location for a 1⅜" dado ½" deep. Cut the marked dadoes as shown on the drawing on the *opposite page*.

3 Next, crosscut the pine piece into two equal lengths. Mark the windshield location on one of the pieces. (The pine piece is still extra

The construction business has never been better. To construct these road-building pieces, build two identical tractors, and add a box to one for the dump truck and a lowboy to the other. Then, use the article starting on page 53 to build the bulldozer. Finally, watch as your youngster's imagination moves mountains.

LOWBOY AND DUMP TRUCK

long, so mark the top of the windshield flush with the top of the dado where shown on the photo *below*. See the Tractor Drawing for size of the window opening). Drill a blade start hole in the center of the windshield, and cut the opening to shape with a coping saw as shown in the photo. Sand or file the windshield edges smooth.

Mark the windshield location, drill a blade start hole, and cut the windshield opening to shape.

4 Apply glue to the mating surfaces, align the dadoes, and clamp the cab parts (A) together face to face. Later, use a sharp chisel to

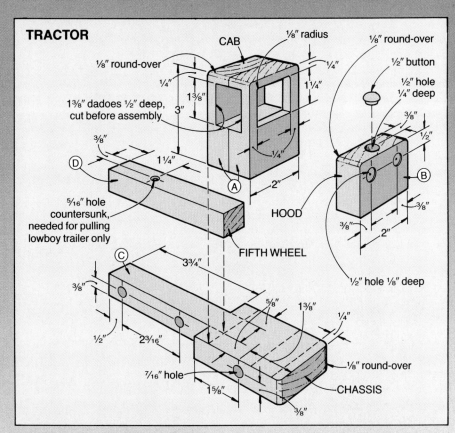

TRACTOR

CAB

⅛" radius

⅛" round-over

½" button

½" hole ¼" deep

⅛" round-over

¼"

¼"

1¾"

1¼"

1⅜"

3"

1⅜" dadoes ½" deep, cut before assembly

¼"

¼"

⅜"

½"

⅜"

2"

⅜"

⅜"

2"

½" hole ⅛" deep

D

⅜"

1¼"

A

2"

B

HOOD

FIFTH WHEEL

⁵⁄₁₆" hole countersunk, needed for pulling lowboy trailer only

C

3¾"

⅜"

⅝"

1⅜"

¼"

½"

2³⁄₁₆"

⅛" round-over

⁷⁄₁₆" hole

1⅝"

⅜"

CHASSIS

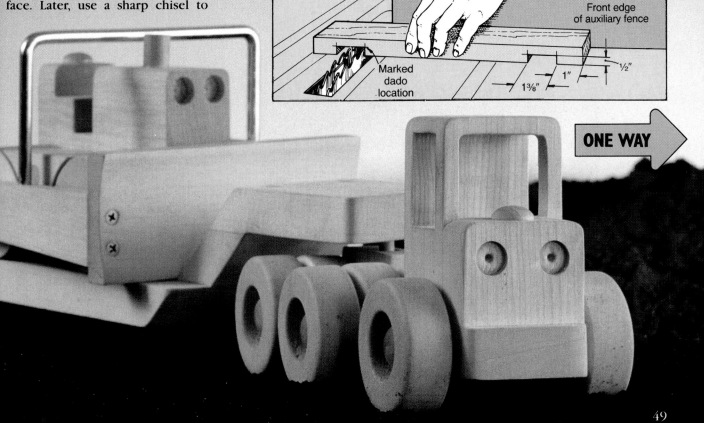

Marked dado location

Front edge of auxiliary fence

½"

1"

1⅜"

ONE WAY

LOWBOY AND DUMP TRUCK

remove all the excess glue, including that inside the cab opening. Trim the top and bottom of the cab lamination to length (3") where dimensioned on the Tractor Drawing. Sand a ⅛" round-over along the sides of the cab top.

5 Cut the hood (B) to size. Sand a ⅛" round-over on the top corners. Then, drill two ½" holes ⅛" deep for the headlights and a ½" hole ¼" deep centered from side to side for the radiator cap in the hood where dimensioned on the Tractor Drawing.

6 With the bottom and edges of the cab and hood flush, glue and clamp them together. (We placed scrap pieces under the clamp heads to prevent denting the soft pine.)

7 Cut the chassis (C) to shape (we did this on a band saw), and sand a ⅛" round-over along the front corners. Mark the axle hole center points on one side of the chassis. Hold the chassis firmly in a hand-screw clamp, and use a drill press to drill the ⁷⁄₁₆" axle holes.

8 Cut the fifth wheel (D) to size. If you plan to build the lowboy later and hitch it to the tractor, drill and countersink a ⁵⁄₁₆" hole where shown on the Tractor Drawing.

9 Leaving a ¼" gap at the front to form the bumper, glue and clamp the cab assembly to the chassis. Later, glue and clamp the fifth wheel on top of the chassis and against the back of the cab. Sand smooth, and glue a ½" button into the radiator cap hole.

Forming the duals

Note: You'll need four inside wheels (E) and six outside wheels (F) for each tractor. In addition, if you make the lowboy, make four inside and four outside wheels.

1 To make enough wheels for one tractor, cut a ¾"-thick piece of pine to 4" wide by 33" long. Use a piece ¾ x 4 x 27" for the lowboy. Starting 3" from either end, mark center points 3" apart down the center of each pine board.

2 With a compass, mark a 2"-diameter circle (1" radius) at each marked center point.

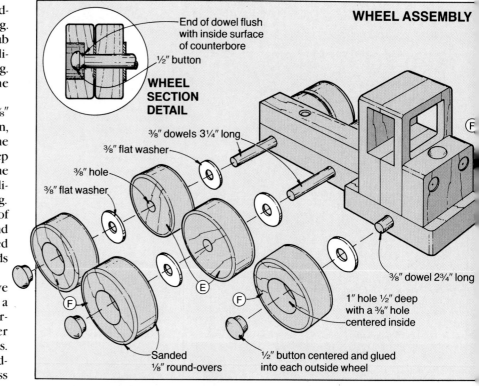

WHEEL ASSEMBLY

End of dowel flush with inside surface of counterbore

½" button

WHEEL SECTION DETAIL

⅜" dowels 3¼" long

⅜" flat washer

⅜" hole

⅜" flat washer

⅜" dowel 2¾" long

1" hole ½" deep with a ⅜" hole centered inside

Sanded ⅛" round-overs

½" button centered and glued into each outside wheel

Mark the wheel center point locations on the pine, and drill holes ½" deep for each outside wheel.

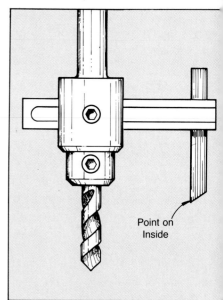

Point on Inside

3 Chuck a 1" Forstner bit into your drill press. Attach a scrap work surface to your drill press table. As shown in the photo *above*, center the bit over a marked center point, and bore a ½" deep hole for each outside wheel (6 outside wheels on the tractor and 4 on the lowboy). We used the stop on our drill press to ensure uniform hole depths.

4 Chuck a circle cutter to your drill press. Turn the cutter blade to cut a perfect wheel where shown on the drawing *above*. Raise the cutter blade ⅝" higher than the bottom of the pilot bit. Center the pilot bit over the centered depression in each 1" hole, and slowly cut the wheels to shape as shown in the photo *above right*.

SANDING THE DUALS

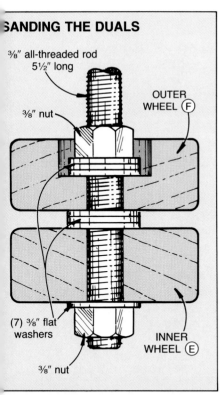

3/8" all-threaded rod 5½" long

OUTER WHEEL (F)

3/8" nut

(7) 3/8" flat washers

INNER WHEEL (E)

3/8" nut

Fasten two wheels at a time to the threaded rod, and sand the wheels smooth. Start with 80-grit sandpaper.

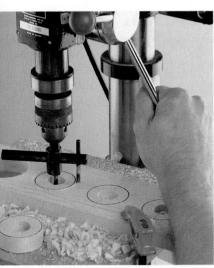

Center the circle-cutter pilot bit over the Forstner-bit depression, and cut the wheels to shape.

5 Center the circle-cutter pilot bit over the remaining marked center points, and cut the four inside wheels to shape.

6 Remove the circle cutter, and chuck a 3/8" twist drill bit into your drill press. Using a handscrew clamp to secure the wheels, enlarge the ¼" axle hole in the center of each wheel to 3/8".

Bill of Materials

Part	Finished Size*			Material	Qty.
	T	W	L		
ONE TRACTOR					
A*	¾"	2"	3"	pine	2
B	¾"	2"	1½"	pine	1
C	¾"	2"	6¾"	pine	1
D	¾"	¾"	4¼"	pine	1
WHEELS FOR ONE TRACTOR					
E	¾"	2" diam.		pine	4
F	¾"	2" diam.		pine	6
DUMP TRUCK BOX					
G	¼"	2¾"	4"	pine	1
H	¼"	2½"	2¾"	pine	1
I	¼"	2¾"	4"	pine	2
J	¼"	¾"	3¼"	pine	1
LOWBOY TRAILER					
K*	¾"	4¼"	11"	pine	1
L*	¾"	2½"	2"	pine	1
M*	¾"	2½"	3¾"	pine	1
N	¾"	¾"	4½"	pine	1

*Parts marked with an * are cut larger initially, and then trimmed to finished size. Please read the instructions before cutting.

Supplies: ½" wood buttons, 3/8" flat washers, 3/8" dowel rod, ¼" dowel rod, 3/8 x 5½" all-thread rod and nuts for work arbor, polyurethane.

7 Cut a piece of 3/8" all-thread rod to 5½" long, and chuck it into your drill press. Attach two wheels at a time to the work arbor where shown on Sanding The Duals Drawing. Starting with 80-grit sandpaper and proceeding through finer grits, sand the wheels smooth. Sand a slight round-over on each wheel as shown in the photo *above*.

Here's how to build the dump-truck box

Note: You'll need ¼" stock to build the box. We resawed 2x4 pine stock on the band saw to 5/16" thick, and then sanded it to ¼" thick.

1 Cut the box bottom (G) and front (H) to size. Now, cut the sides (I) and cab overhang (J) a to rectangular size, mark the radii, and cut the pieces to shape.

DUMP TRUCK BOX

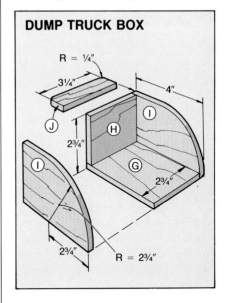

R = ¼"

3¼"

4"

J

I

H

2¾"

I

G

2¾"

2¾"

R = 2¾"

2 Glue and clamp the box bottom and front between the two side pieces, making sure all the edges are flush. Scrape off the excess glue. Later, sand the box smooth, and glue and clamp the cab overhang to the front of the box.

3 Glue and clamp the box to the tractor, flush with the *back* end of the chassis.

DETOUR

LOWBOY AND DUMP TRUCK

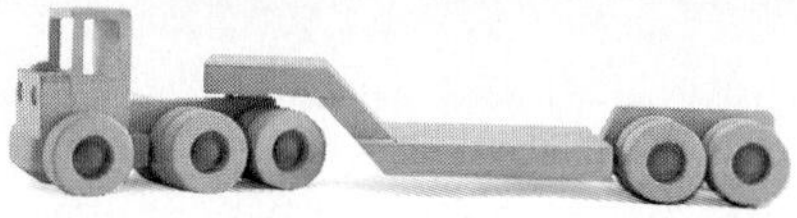

Now, let's construct the lowboy trailer

1 Cut a piece of ¾″ pine to 4¼″ wide by 12″ long for the bed (K). Miter-cut the front end of the bed for an 11″ finished length. Lay out and cut the notches for the rear duals where dimensioned on the Lowboy Trailer Drawing at *right*.

2 Mark the axle hole center, and drill the 7⁄16″ axle holes.

3 Cut a piece of ¾″ pine to 2½″ wide by 12″ long for the gooseneck parts (L, M). With the saw blade 45° from vertical, cut part L to length. From the remaining pine stock, measure 3¾″ from the square end, and miter-cut gooseneck part M to the length shown on the Gooseneck Detail.

4 Using the dimensions on the Lowboy Drawing, glue gooseneck part L to the front end of the bed (K). (We used masking tape to hold part L in position on the bed.) After the glue dries, remove the tape, and glue and tape part M to part L. Let the glue dry and remove the tape.

5 Clamp the lowboy assembly to the top of your workbench. Now, to strengthen the joints, use a brad-point bit (a regular twist bit will tend to wander), to drill two ¼″ holes through M and ½″ into L where shown on the Lowboy Drawing and accompanying Gooseneck Detail. (When drilling the holes, we eyeballed the angle, and placed scrap pieces under the gooseneck to support it.) Flip the assemblies over, and repeat the process to drill through the bed and ½″ into the other end of L.

6 Cut four ¼″ dowels 2″ long. Glue two dowels in place in M and L, and let the glue dry. Next, glue two in place in K and L. After the glue dries, trim and sand the ends flush with the bottom of the bed and the top of the gooseneck.

7 Drill a ¼″ hole ½″ deep centered from side to side in the bottom of gooseneck part M where shown on the Gooseneck Detail. Cut a ¼″ dowel 1⅜″ long, and sand a chamfer on one end of it. With the chamfered end protruding, glue the dowel into the hole.

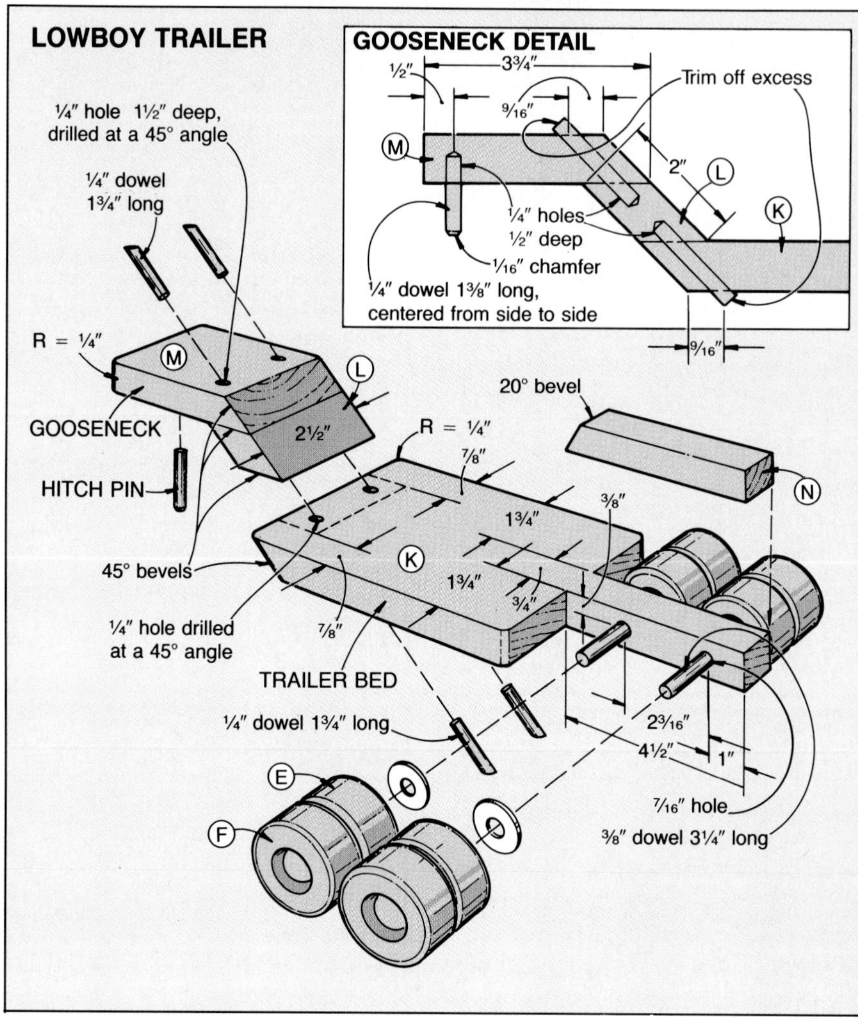

LOWBOY TRAILER
GOOSENECK DETAIL
½″
3¾″
9⁄16″
Trim off excess
M
2″
L
K
¼″ holes
½″ deep
1⁄16″ chamfer
¼″ dowel 1⅜″ long,
centered from side to side
9⁄16″
¼″ hole 1½″ deep,
drilled at a 45° angle
¼″ dowel
1¾″ long
R = ¼″
M
L
20° bevel
GOOSENECK
2½″
R = ¼″
7⁄8″
N
HITCH PIN
⅜″
1¾″
K
45° bevels
1¾″
¾″
¼″ hole drilled
at a 45° angle
7⁄8″
TRAILER BED
¼″ dowel 1¾″ long
2 3⁄16″
4½″
1″
E
F
7⁄16″ hole
⅜″ dowel 3¼″ long

8 Cut part N to size, miter-cutting the front at 20°. Glue and clamp it to the back of the bed (K) with the back of N flush with the back end of the bed.

Attach the duals and apply the finish

1 Cut the tractor and lowboy axles to length from ⅜″ dowel stock as dimensioned on the drawings.

2 Glue one outer wheel onto each dowel axle so that the end of the dowel is flush with the inside of the counterbore where shown on the Wheel Section Detail accompanying the Wheel Assembly Drawing. After the glue dries, slide a ⅜″ flat washer next to the outer tire and an inner tire next to the flat washer. Don't glue the inner tire to the dowel. Slide the axle assembly through the axle hole, and then add a washer, inner tire, and another washer. Glue the outer wheel to the end of the axle dowel, leaving enough free play so the tires turn easily.

3 Follow the procedure in step 2 with two wheels and two washers to form the front-axle assembly.

4 To add the hub caps, set the tractor and lowboy assemblies on their side. Place a dab of glue on the ends of the axle dowels, and glue a ½″ wood button to the end of the dowel. After the glue dries, flip the assemblies over and repeat for the other hub caps.

5 Apply the finish (we used Varathane Professional Clear Finish, an aerosol polyurethane).

STOP

Produced by Marlen Kemmet
Project Design: James R. Downing
Photographs: Bob Calmer
Illustrations: Kim Downing, Bill Zaun

FAT CAT®
BULLDOZER

Every sandbox deserves a bulldozer that can build a road, move a mountain, or dig a valley. And, no matter how lost in the land of make-believe your little construction foreman may be, he'll never forget who built his favorite toy.

Continued →

First, make the chassis and track assembly

1 Using the full-size patterns and carbon paper, transfer the outline of the chassis (A), two track blocks (B), and hole centerpoints onto 1½" stock. (We used 2×6 scrap.)

2 Cut the track blocks to shape with a bandsaw. Rip and crosscut the chassis to its final dimensions. Then, route a ¼" round-over on the chassis where shown on the Exploded View drawing. Cut or dado the notches in the chassis, and drill the ⁷⁄₁₆" axle holes you marked earlier.

3 Lay out and drill the holes for the exhaust stack (½" dowel), gas cap (⅜" wood button), and headlights, using the hole sizes and locations given on the Exploded View drawing. You'll drill the holes in the track block later.

4 With a compass, mark four 2" diameter wheels (C) on 1½" stock. (We used the same scrap stock used for the chassis and track blocks.) Drill a ⅜" hole (we used a bradpoint bit) at the centerpoint of each marked wheel. Carefully cut and sand the four wheels to shape.

5 Cut the front and rear axles to length from ⅜" dowel stock. Glue one wheel onto each axle (the front axle fits flush with the outside face of the front wheels; the back axle protrudes ½" from the outside of each rear wheel).

6 With the chassis on its side (we clamped ours in a woodworker's vise), slide the wheel-axle assemblies into the axle holes. Finally, clamp one track block to the chassis centered between the two wheels, and drill a pair of ⅜" holes through the block and ½" into the chassis. Repeat this process to drill the holes for the other track block. Glue and dowel the track blocks to the dozer. Later, sand the dowels flush with the outside face of each track block.

7 Slide the axle assemblies through the chassis axle holes, and glue a wheel to the other end of each axle. (Be careful not to get the wheels too tight against the chassis. If you get them too tight, the wheels won't turn freely.)

Here's how to shape and attach the dozer blade

1 Cut a piece of ½" stock to 2¼×12" long for the blade (D).

2 To form the curved blade front, start by raising the tablesaw blade ⅛" above the surface of the saw table. Next, set your tablesaw miter gauge at 34° from center. Use this angled setting to position a straightedge (we used a 2×4) next to the blade where shown in the photo *at right*. Clamp the straightedge in place. Start the saw and use push-sticks to move the ½" board across the blade (pushing forward) to cut the cove. Next, raise the blade ⁵⁄₁₆" above the saw-table surface, and make another pass to deepen the cove. (We cut several pieces of scrap stock first to ensure the straightedge

Bill of Materials				
Part	**Finished Size***			**Material**	**Qty.**
	T	**W**	**L**		
A	1½"	3¼"	4¼"	pine	1
B	1½"	1¾"	2⅛"	pine	2
C	1½"	2" diam.		pine	4
D*	½"	2¼"	5¾"	pine	1
E	½"	1¼"	4¾"	pine	2

*Part marked with an * is cut larger initially, and then trimmed to finished size. Please read the instructions before cutting.

Supplies: ½" dowel stock, double-faced tape, ⅜" dowel stock, ¼×13½" cadmium-plated steel rod (available at most hardware stores), 4 — #6×1" flathead wood screws, ⅜" wood button, epoxy, polyurethane or a nontoxic oil finish

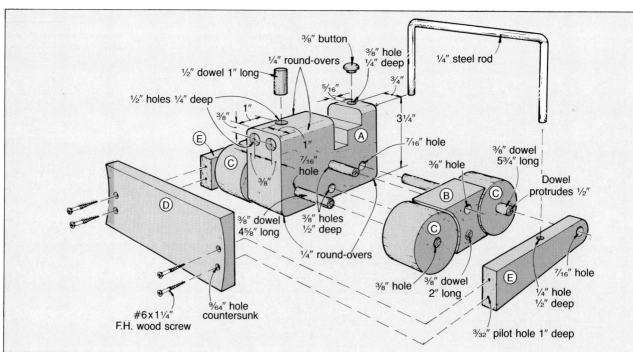

⅜" button
¼" round-overs
⅜" hole ¼" deep
¼" steel rod
½" dowel 1" long
5⁄16"
¾"
½" holes ¼" deep
1"
3¼"
3⁄8"
1"
7⁄16" hole
7⁄16" hole
⅜" hole
⅜" dowel 5¾" long
Dowel protrudes ½"
E
C
A
B
C
C
D
⅜"
⅜" dowel 4⅝" long
⅜" holes ½" deep
¼" round-overs
⅜" hole
⅜" dowel 2" long
E
⁹⁄₆₄" hole countersunk
#6×1¼" F.H. wood screw
7⁄16" hole
¼" hole ½" deep
³⁄₃₂" pilot hole 1" deep

was in the right position to center the cove on the workpiece.) Now, crosscut the blade to finished length.

3 To make the blade arms (E), cut two pieces of ½" stock to 1¼ × 4¾". Using the Blade Arm pattern *lower right*, transfer the blade-arm shape and the 7⁄16" hole location to one of the ½" pieces. Using double-faced tape, adhere the two pieces, with the marked piece on top. Cut the taped-together pieces to shape, and drill a 7⁄16" hole through both pieces for the rear axle. Mark the location, and drill a ¼" hole in the top of each blade arm for the roll bar. Pry the pieces apart, and remove the tape.

4 Drill and countersink four holes through the dozer blade and into the

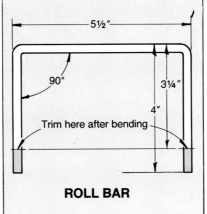

Use the tablesaw and an angled fence to cove the dozer blade.

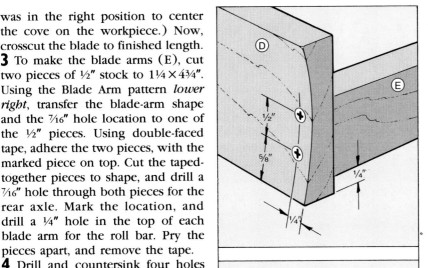

ROLL BAR

blade arm, using the dimensions and hole sizes on the drawing at *left*. (The outside face of the blade arms are flush with the ends of the blade.) Slide the arms onto the rear axle dowel. Glue and screw the blade to the two blade arms.

Form the roll bar and finish the dozer

1 Cut a 13½" length of ¼" steel rod for the roll bar. Mark the locations of the bends with masking tape. Clamp one end of the rod in a vise, and make the bend where shown in the drawing *below left*. Repeat for the other bend.

2 Trim the bottom ends of the roll bar even with a hacksaw. Epoxy the roll bar into the blade arms.

3 Cut the exhaust stack to length. Glue the exhaust stack and 3⁄8" button in place on the chassis. Finally, apply two coats of polyurethane. 🌲

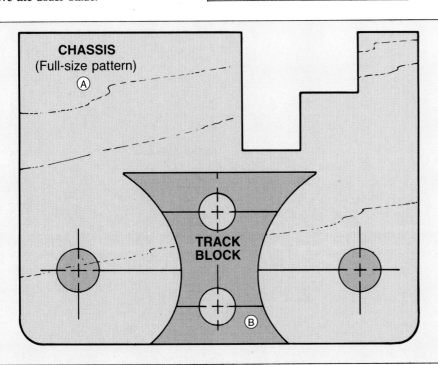

CHASSIS
(Full-size pattern)
Ⓐ

TRACK BLOCK

Ⓑ

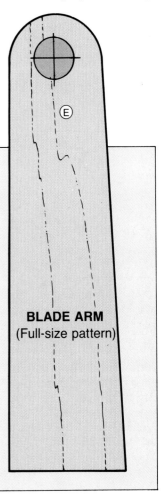

BLADE ARM
(Full-size pattern)

Ⓔ

Project Design: James R. Downing   Photographs: Hopkins Associates; Bob Calmer   Illustrations: Kim Downing; Bill Zaun

WADDLES THE

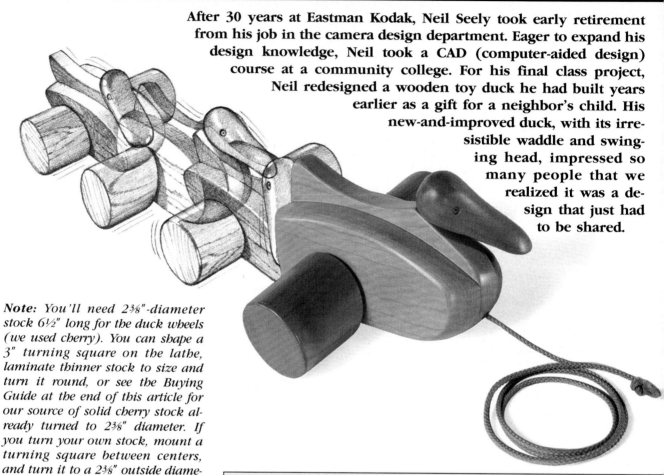

After 30 years at Eastman Kodak, Neil Seely took early retirement from his job in the camera design department. Eager to expand his design knowledge, Neil took a CAD (computer-aided design) course at a community college. For his final class project, Neil redesigned a wooden toy duck he had built years earlier as a gift for a neighbor's child. His new-and-improved duck, with its irresistible waddle and swinging head, impressed so many people that we realized it was a design that just had to be shared.

Note: You'll need 2⅜"-diameter stock 6½" long for the duck wheels (we used cherry). You can shape a 3" turning square on the lathe, laminate thinner stock to size and turn it round, or see the Buying Guide at the end of this article for our source of solid cherry stock already turned to 2⅜" diameter. If you turn your own stock, mount a turning square between centers, and turn it to a 2⅜" outside diameter. Check the diameter as you go with an outside calipers.

Pro"duck"tion begins with the wheel jig

1 From ¾"-thick particleboard or plywood, cut seven pieces 3½" wide by 11" long.
2 Measure and mark a centerpoint on the *top* face of each piece (see the Jig Lamination drawing, *right*).
3 Using a circle cutter chucked in your drill press and a speed of about 250 rpm, test-cut a 2⅜" hole in scrap stock. Check that the 2⅜"-diameter turned stock fits snugly inside the hole in the scrap stock. If the turned stock fits loosely, you will have problems later drill-

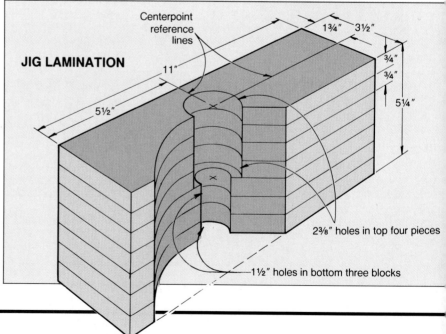

JIG LAMINATION

Centerpoint reference lines

1¾" 3½"
¾"
¾"
11"
5¼"
5½"

2⅜" holes in top four pieces

1½" holes in bottom three blocks

DUCK THE PULL TOY WITH A WADDLE IN ITS WALK

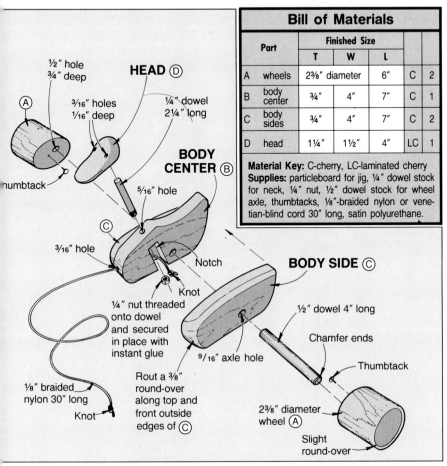

½" hole ¾" deep

HEAD D

A

¾16" holes ¾16" deep

¼" dowel 2¼" long

humbtack

5⁄16" hole

BODY CENTER B

C

¾16" hole

Notch

BODY SIDE C

¼" nut threaded onto dowel and secured in place with instant glue

Knot

9⁄16" axle hole

½" dowel 4" long

Chamfer ends

⅛" braided nylon 30" long

Knot

Rout a ⅜" round-over along top and front outside edges of C

Thumbtack

2⅜" diameter wheel A

2⅜" diameter wheel A

Slight round-over

Bill of Materials

Part		Finished Size				
		T	W	L		
A	wheels	2⅜" diameter		6"	C	2
B	body center	¾"	4"	7"	C	1
C	body sides	¾"	4"	7"	C	2
D	head	1¼"	1½"	4"	LC	1

Material Key: C-cherry, LC-laminated cherry
Supplies: particleboard for jig, ¼" dowel stock for neck, ¼" nut, ½" dowel stock for wheel axle, thumbtacks, ⅛"-braided nylon or venetian-blind cord 30" long, satin polyurethane.

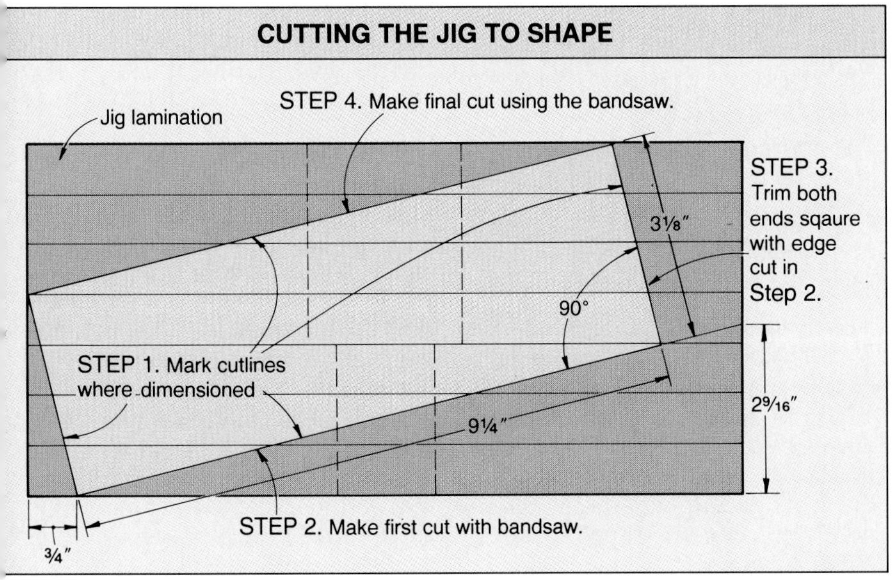

---

ing an accurate axle hole. Adjust the circle cutter if necessary. Center the circle cutter pilot bit directly over the marked centerpoint. Slowly lower the cutter into the stock to cut a 2⅜" hole in four of the jig pieces. Cut or bore a 1½"-diameter hole in the other three pieces.

4 Carefully align the holes where shown on the Jig Lamination drawing, and glue and clamp together the pieces with the 2⅜" holes. (We inserted the 2⅜" turned stock to align the four holes. Once aligned, we clamped together the pieces, removed the turned stock, and wiped off all glue squeeze-out with a damp cloth.) Now, glue and clamp together the three pieces with the 1½" holes, making sure to align the holes. Finally, glue and clamp together the two laminations, with the ends and edges flush.

5 Now, follow the four-step drawing *below left* to mark and cut the jig lamination to shape.

Angle-cut the wheels with the jig

1 If you've turned your own cherry stock for the 2⅜" wheels, crosscut about ⅛" off each end to remove the spur-center and tailstock marks.

CUTTING THE JIG TO SHAPE

Jig lamination

STEP 4. Make final cut using the bandsaw.

3⅛"

STEP 3. Trim both ends sqaure with edge cut in Step 2.

90°

STEP 1. Mark cutlines where dimensioned

9¼"

2⁹⁄16"

STEP 2. Make first cut with bandsaw.

¾"

Insert the turned cherry stock into the hole in the jig, and trim each 2⅜"-diameter duck wheel to length.

Continued

LOCATING THE AXLE AND TACK CENTERPOINTS

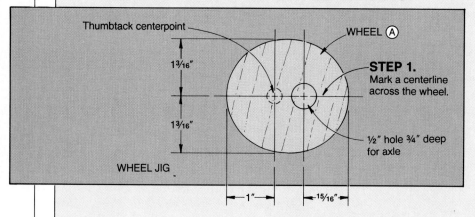

Thumbtack centerpoint

WHEEL Ⓐ

1³⁄₁₆"

1³⁄₁₆"

WHEEL JIG

STEP 1.
Mark a centerline across the wheel.

½" hole ¾" deep for axle

1"

¹⁵⁄₁₆"

STEP 2.
Measure ¹⁵⁄₁₆" from the right edge of wheel, and mark a second reference line across the wheel to locate the centerpoint for axle hole.

STEP 3.
Measure 1" from the left edge of the wheel, and mark a third reference line to locate the centerpoint for thumbtack.

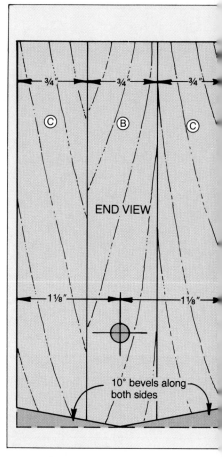

¾"   ¾"   ¾"

Ⓒ   Ⓑ   Ⓒ

END VIEW

1⅛"   1⅛"

10° bevels along both sides

2 Stick the 2⅜" stock all the way into the 2⅜" hole in the jig. To ensure your wheels will end up the right length, the turned stock must bottom out in the 2⅜" hole in the jig. Position the jig between the tablesaw blade and fence where shown in the photo at the bottom of the previous page.

3 Start the saw and cut the turned stock flush with the face of the jig as shown in the above-mentioned photo to form one wheel (A).

4 With the wheel still in•the jig, carefully locate and mark centerpoints for the ½" axle hole and the thumbtack on the cut end of the wheel where shown on the draw-, ing *above*.

5 Chuck a ½" brad-point bit into your drill press and bore ¾" deep into the turned stock as shown in the photo at *right*. (We had our drill press running at 250 rpm.) To prevent the wheel from turning in the jig, feed the bit slowly into the turned stock and back out several times to remove the waste stock. Push a dowel through the 1½" hole in the jig to pop out the wheel.

Center the bit over the mark, and drill a ½" hole ¾" deep in the wheel; then remove the wheel from the jig.

6 Repeat steps 1, 2, 3, 4, and 5 above to form the second cherry wheel (A).

7 Sand a slight round-over along the outside edge of each wheel where shown on the Exploded View drawing.

Now move on to the duck's body

1 From ¾" cherry, cut three pieces 4×7" for the duck body.

2 With carbon paper or by adhering a photocopy of the full-sized Side View Body pattern on the opposite page, transfer the outline, notch, and head-dowel centerline of the body center (B) to one of the 4×7" pieces of cherry. Cut the outline and notch to shape.

3 Transfer the outline for the body side (C) to one of the remaining pieces. Bandsaw and sand it to shape, and use it as a template to mark the outline onto the other body side. Then, cut the outlined piece to shape.

4 Drill a ⁵⁄₁₆" hole through the body center (B) for the head dowel (we used a dowel jig to help align the bit). Now, drill a ³⁄₁₆" hole through the front of the body center for the pull rope where shown on the Body Pattern drawing.

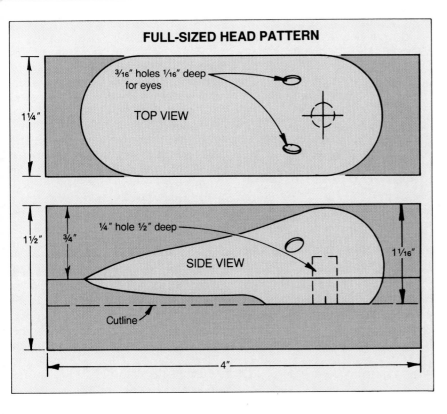

FULL-SIZED BODY PATTERN

7"

90°

Head-dowel centerline

⁵⁄₁₆" hole centered on Ⓑ

Ⓑ

Ⓑ

Ⓒ

4"

90°

Notch cut into Ⓑ only

SIDE VIEW

⁹⁄₁₆" hole

³⁄₁₆" hole centered on Ⓑ

10° bevel along bottom edge of Ⓒ

1"

FULL-SIZED HEAD PATTERN

³⁄₁₆" holes ¹⁄₁₆" deep for eyes

TOP VIEW

1¼"

¼" hole ½" deep

1½" ¾"

SIDE VIEW

1¹⁄₁₆"

Cutline

4"

5 Rout a ⅜" round-over on both body sides (C) where shown on the Exploded View drawing. With the bottom and back edges flush, glue and clamp together the three body pieces.

6 Mark a 10° bevel line on the front and back ends of the body lamination where shown on the drawing *above*. Now, connect the ends of the bevel lines by drawing a line along each side of the lamination. Clamp the duck body upside down in a woodworker's vise and hand-plane or belt-sand the edges to the marked lines.

7 Mark the centerpoint location, and bore a ⁹⁄₁₆" axle hole through the body where shown on the Body Pattern drawing at *top*.

8 Sand the duck body smooth.

Next, cut and shape the duck's head

1 To form the head (D), cut a block to 1¼ × 1½ × 4". If you

Continued

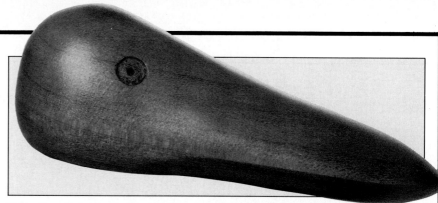

Using the photo above for reference, sand the head and body to shape.

don't have stock this size, laminate ¾″-thick stock and trim it to size, noting the lamination line shown on the Side View of the Head pattern.

2 Transfer the full-sized top and side head patterns to the cherry block. Mark the ¼″ dowel hole centerpoint, and drill the hole where marked. Bandsaw the head side view to shape. Tape together the pieces and cut the top-view pattern to shape as shown *below*, and hand-plane or belt-sand the edges to the marked lines.

3 With a drum or disc sander mounted to your drill press, sand the head to the shape shown in the photo *above*. Then, wrap 100-grit sandpaper around felt or foam, and hand-sand the head smooth. Repeat the hand-sanding operation with 150- and 220-grit sandpaper.

4 Drill a pair of ³⁄₁₆″ holes ¹⁄₁₆″ deep in the duck head for the eyes where shown on the Head Pattern drawing on page 45.

Add the wheels and head to the body

1 From ½″ dowel stock, cut the axle to 4″. For ease of insertion into the wheels, sand a chamfer on each end of the dowel.

2 Push a thumbtack into each wheel where marked. The thumbtack prevents the wheels from rubbing against the sides of the duck body.

3 From ¼″ dowel stock, cut the neck dowel to 2¼″ long. Sand a slight taper on one end of the neck dowel. Hold a ¼″ nut with a pliers. Slowly rotate the tapered end of the neck dowel into the nut to thread the bottom of the dowel. After you've threaded the end of the dowel, remove the nut; we'll add it back after we've applied the finish. Glue the nontapered dowel end into the hole in the duck head.

4 Apply the finish to the duck body, head, and wheels (we left ours unstained and applied two coats of satin polyurethane). Mask the wheel axle to prevent getting any finish on it.

5 Stick the ¼″-diameter, threaded neck dowel through the body. Holding a ¼″ nut with a needle-nosed pliers, thread the nut back onto the tapered end of the dowel. To keep the nut from ever falling off and being accidentally swallowed, add a few drops of instant glue to the nut and dowel.

6 Using white glue to extend working time, glue the axle dowel into the hole in *one* of the wheels. Wipe off excess glue. After the glue dries, stick the axle through the axle hole in the body. Glue the other wheel onto the dowel and immediately (before the glue sets), rotate the second wheel on the dowel until it aligns with the first wheel. Roll the assembly on a flat surface, the duck will roll smoothly and waddle easily once the wheels are aligned. Adjust the wheel alignment if necessary. Remove glue between the wheels and duck body with a damp cloth.

7 Cut a 30″ length of ⅛″ braided nylon. Tie a knot at one end and stick the other end through the rope hole in the duck body. Tie a second knot at the opposite end of the rope. Finally, give Waddles a pull and watch the kids—of all ages—come running.

Buying Guide

● **Turned cherry stock.** 2⅜″ diameter by 6½″ long. Catalog no. AWD01-3. For the current price, contact Adams Wood Products, 974 Forest Dr., Morristown, TN 37814. ♣

Project Design: Neil Seely, Rochester, NY
Photographs: Hopkins Associates
Illustrations: Kim Downing; Bill Zaun

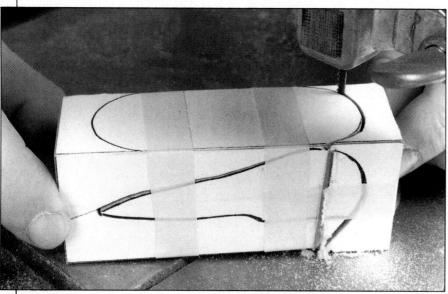

Cut the side-view head pattern to shape. Tape the pieces back together, and cut the top-view pattern.

"TALK OF THE NEIGHBORHOOD"
DOLL STROLLER

When other kids on the block ask your special one where she got this beauty, she'll immediately think of you. It's decidedly stylish, so very practical, and sure get her dolly to those all-important tea parties and neighborhood functions.

First, build the stroller body

1 Cut and edge-join enough ½" pine stock to form two panels — each measuring 12½" square — for the stroller sides (A). Scrape off the excess glue, and use a straightedge to check each panel for flatness. Plane, if necessary.

2 Mark diagonals on one panel to find its center. Mark a 12"-diameter circle on the marked panel (we used trammel points to mark ours). With the marked panel on top, stick the two panels together using double-faced tape. Make sure the grain on both panels runs in the same direction.

Continued

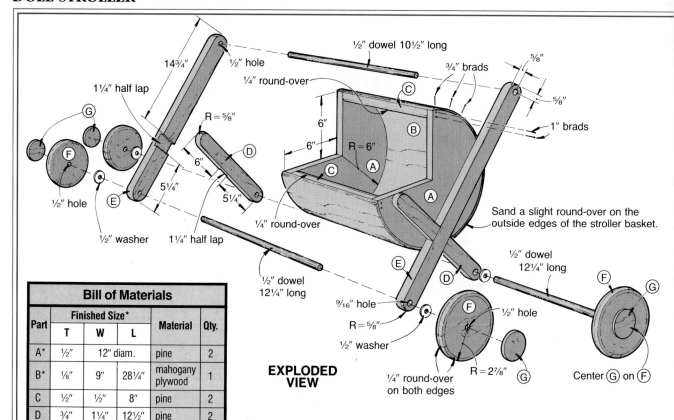

EXPLODED VIEW

Sand a slight round-over on the outside edges of the stroller basket.

Center G on F

Bill of Materials					
Part	**Finished Size***			**Material**	**Qty.**
	T	**W**	**L**		
A*	½"	12" diam.		pine	2
B*	⅛"	9"	28¼"	mahogany plywood	1
C	½"	½"	8"	pine	2
D	¾"	1¼"	12½"	pine	2
E	¾"	1¼"	21¼"	pine	2
F	¾"	5¾" diam.		pine	4
G	⅛"	2½" diam.		mahogany plywood	4

*Parts marked with an * are cut larger initially, and then trimmed to finished size. Please read the instructions before cutting.

Supplies: double-faced tape, paraffin, 1½" dowel 10½" long for handle, 2—½" dowels 12¼" long for axles, 4 — ½" washers, ¾" brads, 1" brads, ½x5" machine bolt with two washers and nuts (for sanding arbor), putty, primer, paint (nontoxic)

3 Mark the stroller-opening cut lines on the two panels, following the five steps outlined in the drawing *below.*

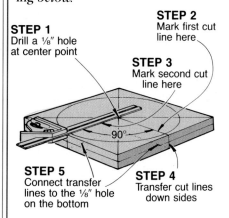

STEP 1
Drill a ⅛" hole at center point

STEP 2
Mark first cut line here

STEP 3
Mark second cut line here

STEP 4
Transfer cut lines down sides

STEP 5
Connect transfer lines to the ⅛" hole on the bottom

4 Using a band saw, cut the taped-together panels to shape, cutting just outside the marked radius and 1" past the 90° cut lines where shown in the drawing *below.* Cutting past the 90° cut lines creates

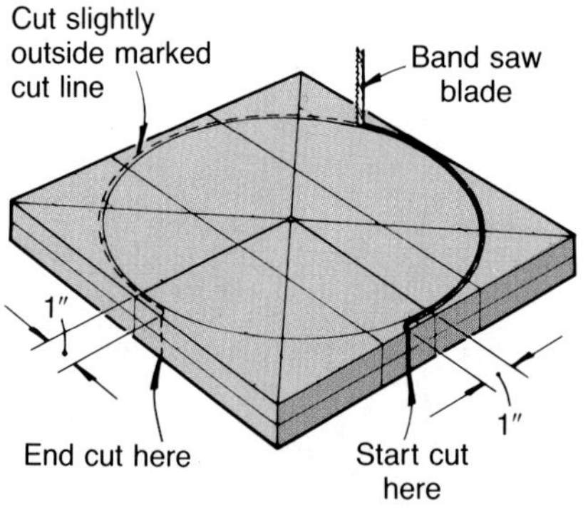

Cut slightly outside marked cut line

Band saw blade

End cut here

Start cut here

notches to capture the plywood surround that you'll fasten to the sides later. Now, sand the panels to the marked radius for the finished shape. Pry the two panels apart, and remove the tape.

5 Cut three 8"-long spacers (we used 1x4s). Align the stroller sides by nailing the first spacer between the corners left square where shown on the following drawing. Now, nail the two remaining spac-

ers between the stroller sides. Let the nail heads protrude; you'll remove the nails later. Clamp the assembly firmly to your workbench as shown in the drawing *below.*

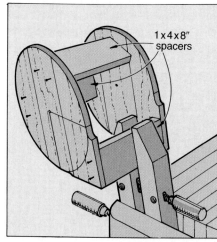

1x4x8" spacers

6 From ⅛" mahogany plywood, rip and crosscut the plywood surround (B) to 9x30". Note that the grain runs crosswise.

7 To make wrapping the plywood around the sides easier, sponge the outside face of the plywood with warm water. Starting the plywood in the notches cut earlier with the band saw, wrap the plywood around the stroller sides, gluing and nailing as you work as shown in photo A. (We attached a clamp to the free end of the plywood to help hold it down as we nailed it in place.) Let the glue dry. Later, remove the 1 x 4 spacers.

8 Using a fine-tooth handsaw, cut along the 90° cut lines to form the stroller body opening.

9 Cut the two rails (C) to size. Rout a ¼″ round-over along one edge on both. Glue and clamp each rail in position between the stroller sides, flush against the plywood. Sand a slight round-over on the outside edges of the stroller basket.

Now, for the frame

1 Cut the frame parts (D, E) to size. Refering to the Exploded-View Drawing at *left*, mark a ⅝″ radius and hole locations on the ends of each piece. Then, mark the location of the half-lap joints on each frame part. Mount a dado blade to your table or radial arm saw, and cut a 1¼″-wide half lap in each piece where marked. Cut the radiused ends to shape.

2 Drill ⁹⁄₁₆″ holes for the axles and ½″ holes for the handle in the frame parts. (We used double-faced tape to stick the pieces together, and then drilled the holes through both at one time.) Sand the frame parts smooth.

3 Glue each frame assembly together, checking for square.

The axles and wheels come next

1 Cut four 6″-square pieces from ¾″ pine stock for the wheels. Draw diagonals to find center, and mark a 2⅞″ radius on each. Cut the wheels to shape.

2 To true up the wheels, start by drilling a ½″ hole through each at the marked center point. Fasten the four wheels on a ½ x 5″ machine bolt with flat washers on the top and bottom as shown in photo B. Chuck this assembly to your drill press, and sand smooth. (We used a half-sheet of 60-grit sandpaper applied to particleboard with spray-

Moisten the plywood with warm water, start it in the cut notch, and then glue and nail it as you wrap it around the stroller sides.

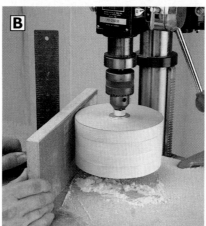

Sand all four wheels round at the same time on the drill press.

on adhesive and held at 90° to the table with a try square. We positioned the drill press belt to run it at the slowest speed possible.)

3 Rout a ¼″ round-over on both edges of each wheel (we routed ours with a table-mounted router).

4 To make the decorative hubcaps (G) mark four 1¼″-radius circles on ⅛″ plywood. Cut the hubcaps to shape, and sand them smooth. Center and glue one of the hubcaps to each wheel.

5 Cut the push bar and two axles from ½″ dowel stock. Use the dimensions given on the Exploded-View Drawing.

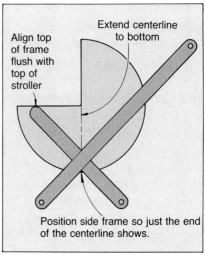

Align top of frame flush with top of stroller

Extend centerline to bottom

Position side frame so just the end of the centerline shows.

Final assembly and finishing

1 Glue and nail the side frames to the stroller body using the drawing *above* as a guide. Glue the push bar in position.

2 Fill any voids with putty and finish-sand the entire stroller. Apply a primer coat, then paint as desired.

3 Apply paraffin to the inside surface of all axle holes. Slide the axles through the holes, slip a washer on each axle end, then glue a wheel to the end of each axle. ♣

Project Design: James R. Downing
Photographs: William Hopkins; Bob Calmer; Jim Kascoutas
Illustrations: Kim Downing; Bill Zaun

all aboard PLAYTIME EXPRESS

Looking for just the right gift for a favorite youngster? If so, you've just struck it rich because this pint-sized plaything will soon be one of that child's favorite possessions. We scaled down the size of the locomotive and cars so that even toddlers can maneuver them easily. And because young "engineers" can sometimes get overly energetic when operating trains, we designed the project to stand up to plenty of playful abuse.

Note: You'll need some thin stock for this project. You can either re-saw or plane thicker stock to the correct thickness.

Start with the locomotive

1 To make the locomotive chassis (A), cut ¾″ maple to the size listed in the Bill of Materials. Then, drill a ³⁄₃₂″ pilot hole ¼″ deep and ¼″ from one end for the coupler screw where shown on the Locomotive Exploded View drawing.

2 To form the boiler (B), cut two pieces of ¾″ maple to 1½×12″. Glue and clamp them face-to-face, with the edges flush. Later, sand the block smooth, and use your router table to rout a ⅜″ round-over along the first 3″ of the top two edges. Cut a 2⅝″ piece from the rounded-over portion of the block, and set aside the remainder for the passenger car and caboose. Now, glue and clamp the boiler flush with the front of the chassis and centered from side to side.

3 Cut the boiler front plate (C) to 2×2½″ from ½″ maple stock. Cut ½″ radii on the top two corners. Sand the boiler front plate smooth, and glue it to the front of the chassis and boiler.

4 Using ⅜″ maple, cut the two sides (D), the front (E), and the bottom (F) of the cab to size. Drill a 1¼″ "window" in each side where shown in the Side View drawing. Then, glue all the cab pieces together where shown in the locomotive Exploded View drawing. Sand the edges smooth, and glue the cab to the chassis, directly behind the boiler.

5 Drill a ⅜″ hole ½″ deep 1″ back from the front end of the boiler for the smokestack dowel. Next, mark the location of the three axle holes with a center punch or a 6d nail (see the Side View drawing for placement). Then, *carefully* drill a ⁹⁄₃₂″ hole all the way through the chassis (the indentation will help prevent the bit from wandering when you start the hole).

6 Cut a piece of ½″ walnut to 2½×10″ for the roof (G). Then, cut a 45° bevel along one end, and cut the roof to finished length (3¼″). Glue the roof to the top of the cab (it should overlap the front by ¼″ and each side by ⅝″).

7 To form the cowcatcher (H), start by cutting 10 pieces of ¼″-thick maple to 2¼×10″. Laminate them face-to-face, removing any

Continued

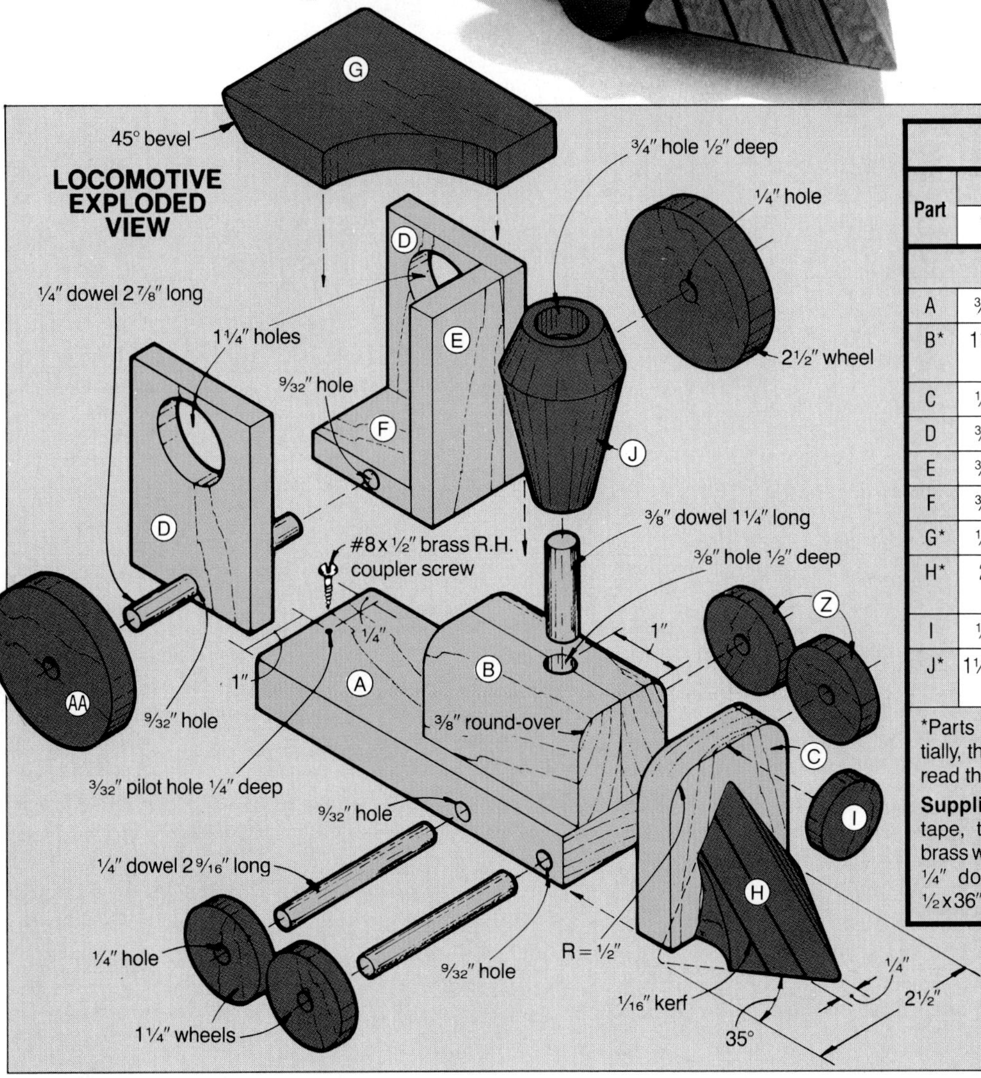

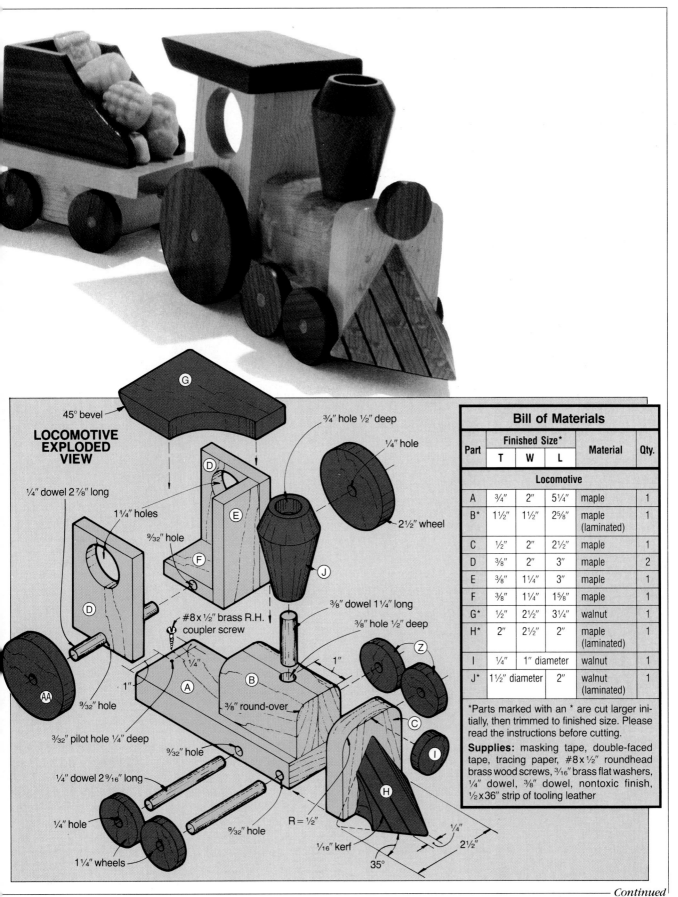

LOCOMOTIVE EXPLODED VIEW
45° bevel
G
3/4" hole 1/2" deep
1/4" hole
D
1 1/4" holes
E
2 1/2" wheel
1/4" dowel 2 7/8" long
9/32" hole
F
J
D
3/8" dowel 1 1/4" long
#8 x 1/2" brass R.H. coupler screw
3/8" hole 1/2" deep
Z
1/4"
1"
1"
B
A
AA
3/8" round-over
9/32" hole
C
3/32" pilot hole 1/4" deep
9/32" hole
I
1/4" dowel 2 9/16" long
H
1/4" hole
9/32" hole
R = 1/2"
1/4"
2 1/2"
1/16" kerf
1 1/4" wheels
35°

Bill of Materials

Part	Finished Size*			Material	Qty.
	T	W	L		
Locomotive					
A	3/4"	2"	5 1/4"	maple	1
B*	1 1/2"	1 1/2"	2 5/8"	maple (laminated)	1
C	1/2"	2"	2 1/2"	maple	1
D	3/8"	2"	3"	maple	2
E	3/8"	1 1/4"	3"	maple	1
F	3/8"	1 1/4"	1 5/8"	maple	1
G*	1/2"	2 1/2"	3 1/4"	walnut	1
H*	2"	2 1/2"	2"	maple (laminated)	1
I	1/4"	1" diameter		walnut	1
J*	1 1/2" diameter		2"	walnut (laminated)	1

*Parts marked with an * are cut larger initially, then trimmed to finished size. Please read the instructions before cutting.

Supplies: masking tape, double-faced tape, tracing paper, #8 x 1/2" roundhead brass wood screws, 3/16" brass flat washers, 1/4" dowel, 3/8" dowel, nontoxic finish, 1/2 x 36" strip of tooling leather

Continued

squeeze-out after it forms a tough skin. Plane or sand the edges of the lamination smooth.

8 Referring to the three-step drawing *below*, follow steps 1 and 2 to shape the front of the cowcatcher. Next, clamp the stock in a vise, with the beveled end up, and sand the beveled surfaces smooth. Cut ¹⁄₁₆"-deep accent kerfs with a fine-toothed handsaw along the glue joints on the front of the cowcatcher. Then, follow step 3 to cut the parts to its 2" finished length. Glue the cowcatcher in place, centered on the boiler front plate and flush with the bottom of the chassis.

9 Make the headlamp (I) by cutting a 1"-diameter plug from ¼"-thick walnut scrap. If you don't have a plug cutter, rough-cut the part with a bandsaw or scrollsaw, and sand the edges smooth. Glue the headlamp to the boiler plate, centered over the cowcatcher and extending ½" above the top edge of the boiler plate.

The smokestack comes next

I To make the smokestack (J), start by laminating two ¾ × 1½ × 6" pieces of walnut face-to-face. Later,

crosscut the ends square, and draw diagonals on one end to find the center. Now, draw a 1½"-diameter circle with a compass on this same end, and clamp the block in your vise. Using the circle as a guide, hand-plane the block to a rough cylinder shape.

2 Crosscut a piece 2" long from this block to make the turning stock for

the smokestack. Use a handscrew to secure the block, and use your drill press to bore a ¾" hole ½" deep in one end (where shown on the Locomotive Side View drawing *below*). Replace the ¾" bit with a ⅜" bit, and drill the hole entirely through the walnut block.

3 Pass a ⅜ × 3" bolt through the block, with its head inside the ¾"

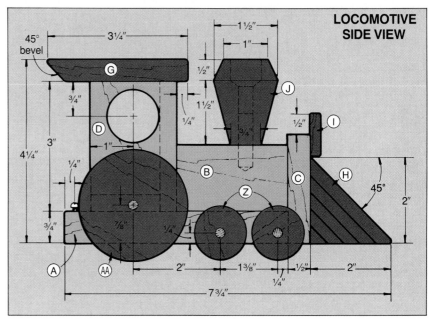

LOCOMOTIVE SIDE VIEW

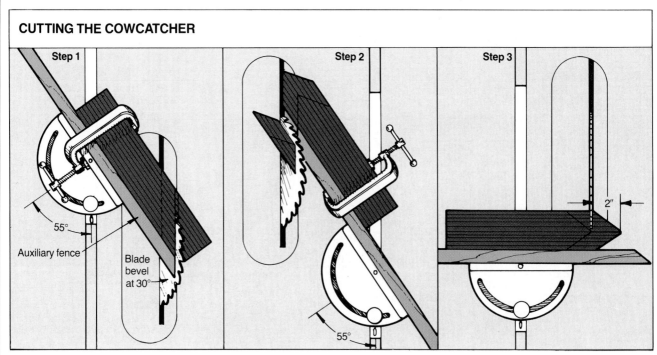

CUTTING THE COWCATCHER

hole, and secure the bolt with a nut. Chuck the protruding end of the bolt in your drill press. (The smokestack will be upside down.)

4 With the drill press running at a medium speed (800-1,000 rpm) "turn" the wood to shape, using a Surform Plane or wood rasp. Work the tool against the spinning wood as shown in the photo, *right*. Shape

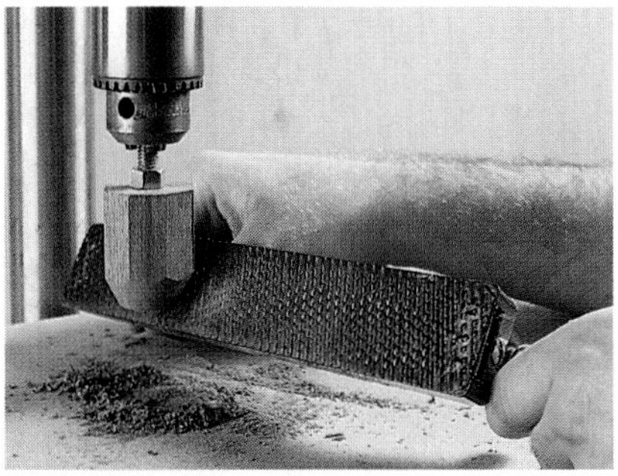

the smokestack to the dimensions indicated on the Side View drawing, and sand it smooth.

5 Remove the smokestack from the drill press. Remove the nut and bolt, and glue the smokestack in place with a 3/8 × 1¼" dowel.

And now for the railcars

1 Rip and crosscut a piece of ½" maple to 2½ × 21" for the floors of the coal car, flat car, passenger car, and the caboose. Then, crosscut two pieces (K) to 4½" and two pieces (L) to 5" from the strip.

2 Attach a piece of masking tape to all floor parts, and label them "coal car", "flat car", etc. Drill 3/32" pilot holes ¼" deep and ¼" from both ends for the coupler screws in floors (K, L) where shown on the different drawings. *Notice* that the front hole for the coupler in the coal car is drilled from the *underside* of the floor.

3 To make the chassis for each car, start by cutting two pieces of ¾" maple to 1 × 15" and one piece of ½" maple 1 × 15". Glue and clamp the three pieces together face-to-face with the ½" strip sandwiched between the ¾" strips. Scrape off the excess glue, and sand or plane the top and bottom surfaces of the lamination smooth. Cut two pieces (M) 3" long and two pieces (N) 3½" long from the lamination.

4 Drill a 9/32" hole for the wheel axles in each chassis after marking the centerpoint location of each hole with a center punch.

5 Center each floor over its corresponding chassis (part K to M and part L to N), then glue and clamp the parts together.

6 To construct the coal car, cut the sides (O) and back (P) to the sizes listed in the Bill of Materials. Stick the two sides together face-to-face using double-faced tape. Use carbon paper to transfer the full-sized side pattern shown *left*, onto the

Continued

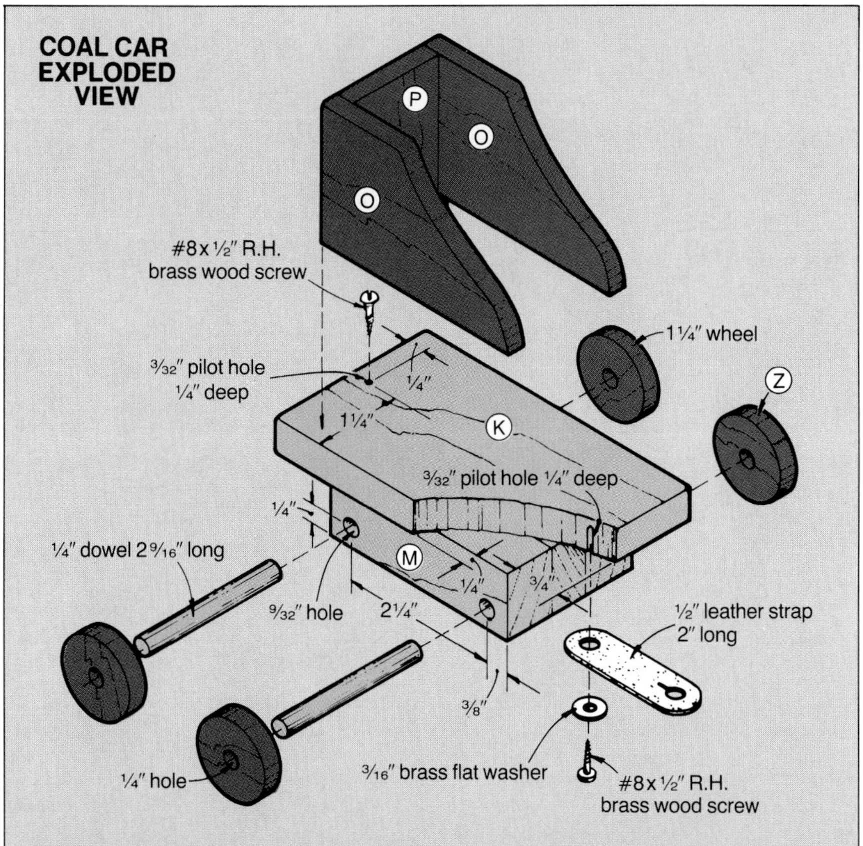

COAL CAR EXPLODED VIEW
P
O
O
#8 x ½" R.H. brass wood screw
3/32" pilot hole ¼" deep
¼"
1¼"
K
3/32" pilot hole ¼" deep
1¼" wheel
Z
¼"
¼" dowel 2 9/16" long
M
¼"
¾"
9/32" hole
2¼"
½" leather strap 2" long
3/8"
3/16" brass flat washer
#8 x ½" R.H. brass wood screw
¼" hole

Part	Finished Size*			Material	Qty.
	T	W	L		
Coal Car					
K*	½"	2½"	4½"	maple	1
M*	1"	2"	3"	maple (laminated)	1
O	¼"	2"	3½"	walnut	2
P	¼"	1½"	2"	walnut	1

Bill of Materials

*Parts marked with an * are cut larger initially, then trimmed to finished size. Please read the instructions before cutting.

Supplies: same as locomotive on page 65

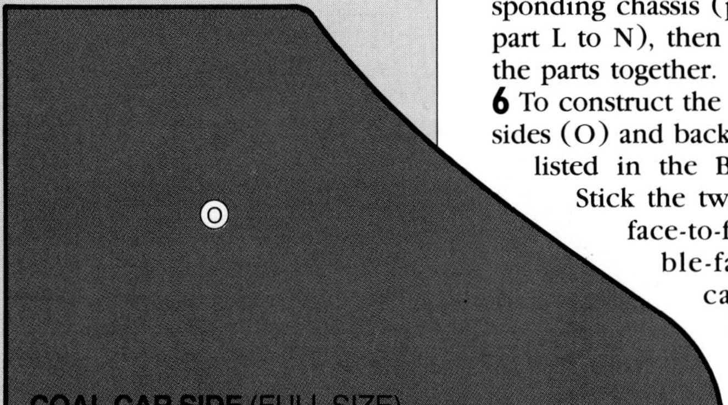

O

COAL CAR SIDE (FULL SIZE)

PLAYTIME EXPRESS

top walnut piece. Cut the sides to shape, sand the contoured edges, and separate, remove the tape. Glue the sides and back together. Next, center and glue this assembly onto the coal car floor (K).

7 Cut the sides (Q) and end (R) to size for the flat car shown at *right*. Cut the front end of each side to shape, and sand. Center the sides and end over the floor of the car, and glue and clamp them in place.

8 To fashion the passenger car, first cut a 3¾"-long car body (S) from the lamination you made earlier for the boiler. Next, drill the three 1" window holes in it (refer to the Passenger Car drawing for correct positioning). Cut the roof (T) to size from ½" walnut. Cut the cupola (U) to size from ½" maple. Fit a ½" beading bit in your table-mounted router, and rout a bead along the top edge of the cupola, using a hand-screw to hold the stock as shown in the photo *below*. Center the car body, roof, and cupola over the floor of the car, and glue and clamp the parts together.

9 For the caboose, cut the car body (V) to size from the remainder of the boiler/passenger car body lamination. Then, drill ⅞" "windows" where shown in the Caboose drawing, *far right*. Cut the parts for the roof (W) and the cupola (X, Y) to the sizes listed in the Bill of Materials. Center, then glue and clamp the car body to the floor. Attach the roof of the body the same way. Then, glue and clamp the cupola to the roof in the position shown in the Caboose drawing.

10 You'll need to make twenty 1¼" wheels (Z), and two 2½" wheels

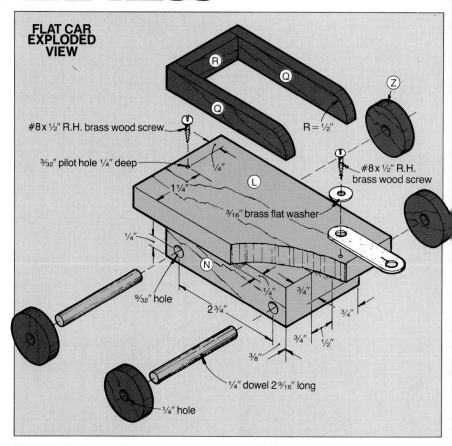

FLAT CAR EXPLODED VIEW

#8 x ½" R.H. brass wood screw
³⁄₃₂" pilot hole ¼" deep
R = ½"
#8 x ½" R.H. brass wood screw
¼"
1¼"
³⁄₁₆" brass flat washer
¼"
⁹⁄₃₂" hole
2¾"
¾"
¾"
¾"
¾"
½"
³⁄₈"
¼" dowel 2⁹⁄₁₆" long
¼" hole

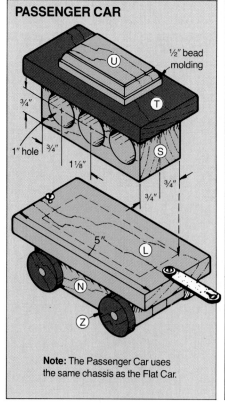

PASSENGER CAR

½" bead molding
¾"
1" hole | ¾"
1⅛"
¾"
¾"
5"

Note: The Passenger Car uses the same chassis as the Flat Car.

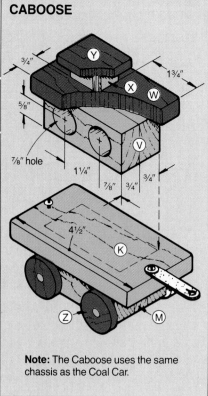

CABOOSE

¾"
1¾"
⅝"
⅞" hole
1¼"
⅞" | ¾" | ¾"
4½"

Note: The Caboose uses the same chassis as the Coal Car.

Bill of Materials

Part	Finished Size* T	Finished Size* W	Finished Size* L	Material	Qty.
Flat Car					
L*	½"	2½"	5"	maple	1
N*	1"	2"	3½"	maple (laminated)	1
Q	¼"	½"	3½"	walnut	2
R	¼"	½"	1½"	walnut	1
Passenger Car					
L*	½"	2½"	5"	maple	1
N*	1"	2"	3½"	maple (laminated)	1
S*	1½"	1½"	3¾"	maple (laminated)	1
T	½"	2¼"	4½"	walnut	1
U	½"	1½"	2½"	maple	1
Caboose					
K*	½"	2½"	4½"	maple	1
M*	1"	2"	3"	maple (laminated)	1
V*	1½"	1¼"	3"	maple (laminated)	1
W	½"	2¼"	3¾"	walnut	1
X	½"	¾"	1"	maple	1
Y	¼"	1¼"	1½"	walnut	1
Wheels					
Z	¼"	1¼" diameter		walnut	20
AA	⅜"	2½" diameter		walnut	2

*Parts marked with an * are cut larger initially, then trimmed to finished size. Please read the instructions before cutting.
Supplies: same as locomotive on page 65

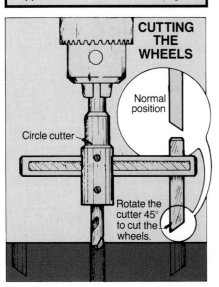

CUTTING THE WHEELS

Circle cutter

Normal position

Rotate the cutter 45° to cut the wheels.

(AA) to get this train rolling. If you use a circle cutter like we did (see the Buying Guide at the end of the article for details), first rotate the blade of the circle cutter to make an inside cut as shown in the drawing and photo *below*. Then, cut the wheels to size.

ll Cut the axles to length (10 at 2⁹⁄₁₆" and one at 2⅞") from ¼" dowel stock. *Do not* glue the wheels to the axles yet.

Finishing and final assembly

l Finish-sand all surfaces of the train. Sand a slight round-over on all edges and corners for safe, smooth handling.

2 Apply two or more coats of a nontoxic clear finish. (We used salad bowl finish; see the Buying Guide for ordering details.)

3 Glue one wheel on each axle so the end of the axle dowel is flush with the outside surface of the wheel. Wipe off any excess glue, and insert the axles through the holes in the various cars. Being careful not to glue the axle or

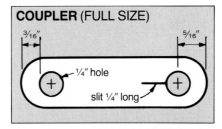

COUPLER (FULL SIZE)

3⁄16" 5⁄16"

¼" hole

slit ¼" long

wheel to the chassis, glue the other wheels onto the other end of each axle. Allow ¹⁄₁₆" play for clearance.

4 Cut the leather couplers to size (see the full-sized drawing *below*). Then, punch or drill ¼" holes spaced where shown. If you don't have a punch, cut a 2" length of ¼" thin-walled brass tubing (available at local hobby stores) and file a sharp bevel around the outside rim of one end. Mount the tube in your drill press and "drill" out the holes. Or, use a ¼" brad-point bit (be sure to clamp the leather firmly to a scrap piece of wood with a hand-screw clamp before drilling—the leather has a tendency to rotate with the bit. Cut a ¼"-long slit next to one of the holes in each coupler. Then, cut each end to shape with a utility knife.

5 Fasten a coupler to the front of each car with a #8 × ½" brass wood screw and a flat washer. Then, drive a screw of the same size into the pilot holes at the rear of each car.

Buying Guide

● **Circle cutter.** Adjustable from 1" to 6", ⅜" chuck, hex wrench included, cuts wheels as well as circles. For the current price, contact Meisel Hardware Spec., P.O. Box 70, Mound, MN, 55364-0070. Or call 800-441-9870 or 612/471-8550 to order.

● **Salad bowl finish.** Nontoxic clear finish, application ease of an oil finish and the sheen building and resistance properties of a varnish. One quart, catalog no. 9896. For the current price, contact Meisel Hardware Spec. at the address listed above.

● **Leather strip.** ½ × 44", Tandy catalog no. 4486. Write Tandy Leather Company, P.O. Box 2934WD, Fort Worth, TX 76113, for the store nearest you. 🌳

Produced by Marlen Kemmet; Yosh Sugiyama
Project Design and Illustrations: Kim Downing; Bill Zaun
Photographs: Hopkins Associates; Jim Kascoutas

Dolls are a lot like young kids. They HATE to go to bed. But almost to the doll, they like to swing, eat, and play school. You can make things even more fun by building one or more of these pint-sized furniture pieces. We know someone else who'll think you're pretty great, too.

SMILE AWHILE
DOLL FURNITURE

SWEETHEART OF A SWING

1 Cut the frame uprights (A) and the cross members (B) to size plus 1″ in length. Mark and miter-cut the angled ends of A to finished length (use the Angle Guide as a reference). Glue and clamp the two upright assemblies. (We used temporary glue blocks tacked in position with hotmelt glue as shown in the Exploded View drawing to anchor the clamps.)

2 Bore four 1″-diameter holes ¼″ deep where indicated in the Exploded View drawing. Then, resaw some birch scrap stock to ¼″ and use a plug cutter to make two surface splines (C). (These add strength to the joint.) Glue the surface splines in the two outside holes, and sand smooth after the glue dries.

3 Lay the frames on a flat surface, and position the cross members (B) under them, 9″ up from the bottom of the frames. Trace the angle to be cut on both ends of each B. Miter-cut the ends. Glue the B's between the uprights and, after

Continued

Bill of Materials

Part	Finished Size*			Material	Qty.
	T	W	L		
A*	¾″	1¼″	24″	birch	4
B*	¾″	1″	9⅜″	birch	2
C	1″ diam.		¼″	dowel	2
D	1″ diam.		14½″	dowel	1
E	¾″	8⅛″	8¾″	birch	1
F*	¾″	¾″	8½″	birch	2
G	¾″	1⅜″	7⅜″	birch	1
H	¼″ diam.		¾″	dowel	2
I	⅜″ diam.		9⅜″	dowel	2
J	¾″	1¼″	9½″	birch	2
K	¾″ diam.		5½″	dowel	2

*Some parts are cut larger initially, then trimmed to the finished size. Please read instructions before cutting.

Supplies: #8×1¼″ flathead wood screws, #8×1½″ flathead wood screws, 48″ of #14 weldless jack and single coil chain, 8—medium screw eyes, 2—¼×2″ hanger bolts with nuts and washers, 2—¾″ key rings, clear finish.

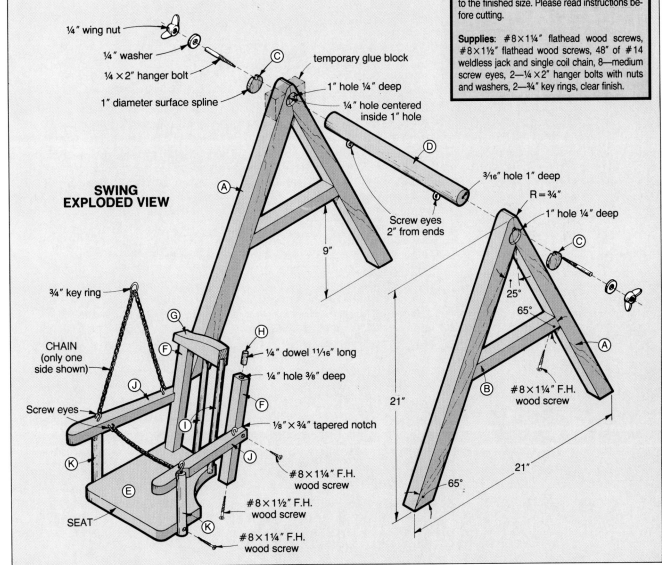

SWING EXPLODED VIEW

¼″ wing nut

¼″ washer

¼×2″ hanger bolt

1″ diameter surface spline

temporary glue block

1″ hole ¼″ deep

¼″ hole centered inside 1″ hole

3/16″ hole 1″ deep

R = ¾″

1″ hole ¼″ deep

Screw eyes 2″ from ends

9″

25°

65°

¾″ key ring

CHAIN (only one side shown)

¼″ dowel 11/16″ long

¼″ hole ⅜″ deep

Screw eyes

⅛″ × ¾″ tapered notch

#8 × 1¼″ F.H. wood screw

21″

#8 × 1¼″ F.H. wood screw

SEAT

#8 × 1½″ F.H. wood screw

#8 × 1¼″ F.H. wood screw

65°

65°

21″

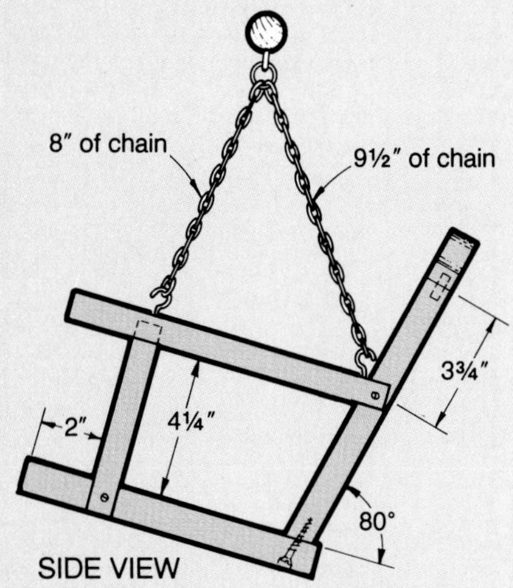
8″ of chain
9½″ of chain
3¾″
2″
4¼″
80°
SIDE VIEW

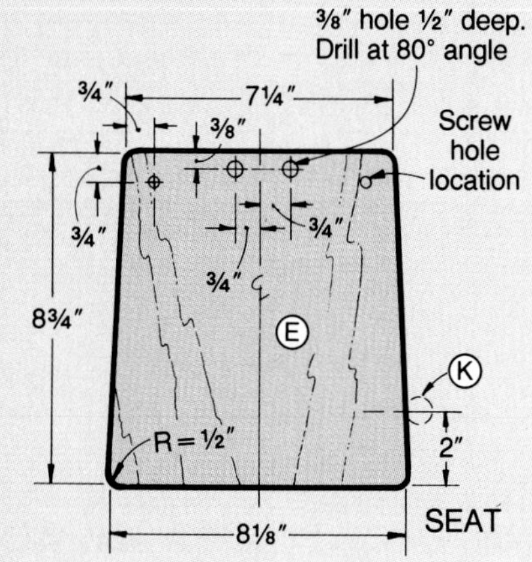
⅜″ hole ½″ deep.
Drill at 80° angle
¾″
7¼″
⅜″
Screw hole location
¾″
¾″
¾″
8¾″
E
K
R=½″
2″
8⅛″
SEAT

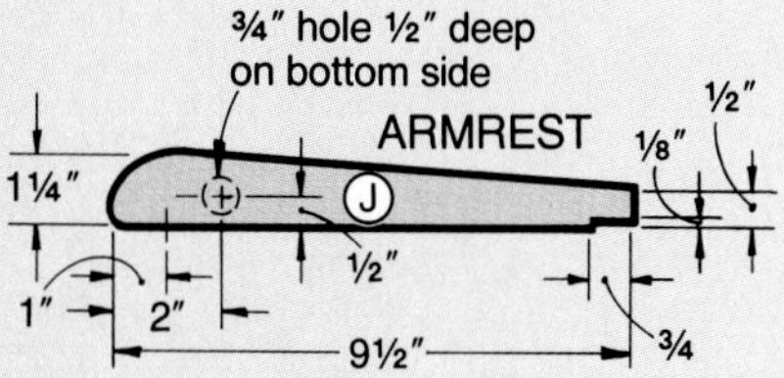
¾″ hole ½″ deep on bottom side
ARMREST
½″
⅛″
1¼″
J
½″
1″
2″
9½″
¾

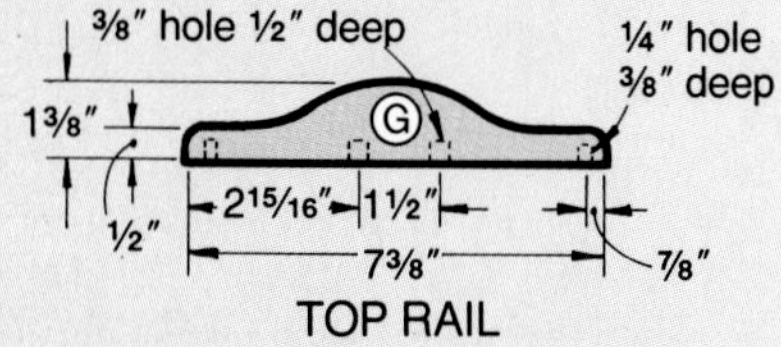
⅜″ hole ½″ deep
¼″ hole ⅜″ deep
1⅜″
G
½″
2¹⁵⁄₁₆″
1½″
7⅜″
⅞″
TOP RAIL

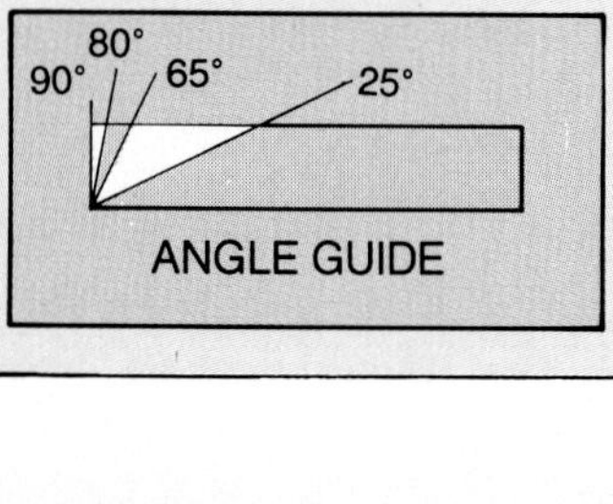
80°
90°
65°
25°
ANGLE GUIDE

the glue dries, toe-screw a #8×1¼″ screw at each joint. Round the top of the frames by cutting or sanding.

4 Cut the top rail (D) to length. Drill a ¼″ hole through the center of the remaining two 1″ holes to accommodate a ¼×2″ hanger bolt. Using this hole as drilling guide, insert D into the hole and drill a 3⁄16″ pilot hole 1″ deep into the ends of D to receive the wood-thread end of the hanger bolt. Attach D to the frames with the hanger bolts, washers, and wing nuts.

5 Cut the chair seat (E) and the chair back parts (F, G, H, I) to size. [Cut the seat (E) and the top rail (G) to the shape indicated in the Parts View drawing.]

6 Lay out, mark, and drill holes in the seat and the top rail (G) where indicated in the same drawing. Also bevel one end of each of the chair back supports (F) at 80°, and drill a ¼″ hole ⅜″ deep in the center of the squared-off end of each.

7 Glue and clamp the chair back assembly (F, G, H, I) to the seat (E). (We used two Jorgensen sliding head-type clamps.)

8 Cut the armrests (J) to the shape shown in the Parts View drawing. Lay out, mark, and drill a ¾″ hole ½″ deep in the bottom of each armrest (refer to the drawing for positioning). Then, cut the armrest supports (K) to length, and glue and clamp them into the holes in the armrests. After the glue dries, position the armrest assembly (J, K) against the seat and the chair back supports (F) where shown in the Seat Side View. (You may need an extra pair of hands to help out here.) Drill the pilot holes where shown, and screw the armrest assembly to the seat and chair back.

9 Install the screw eyes and attach the key rings and chain. Adjust the length of the chain so that the back of the seat rests slightly lower than the front. Sand all the parts smooth and apply a clear finish.

NOT-VERY HIGH CHAIR

Note: *Building the high chair requires several angled holes. While you could measure and drill each hole as angled in the drawings, we simply "eyeballed" the angles when drilling the holes.*

1 Cut the legs (A) to length. Then, cut a tenon on one end of each leg. To do this, set the fence on the tablesaw ⅜″ away from the side of the saw blade farthest from the fence. Now, raise the blade ¼″ above the table surface. One at a time, place the legs against the miter gauge with the end to be cut against the rip fence; slide the dowel and miter gauge forward. Once the dowel is over the center of the moving blade, *slowly* roll the dowel to cut a ¼″ tenon ⅜″ long. Next, sand a chamfer on the bottom of each leg.

2 Cut the stretchers (B, C) to length from ⅜″ dowel. Cut the seat (D) to the shape shown the Seat drawing. Drill four angled ¼″ holes ⅜″ deep in the seat bottom for legs, where shown on the drawings (the hole locations are dimensioned on the Seat drawing while the angles are given on the Front and Side View drawings). Drill ⅜″ holes ⅜″ deep in the legs for B and C (see the Front and Side View drawings for location).

3 Cut the chair back uprights (E), top rail (F), armrests (G), dowel pins (H), back supports (I), and armrest supports (J) to length. Drill a ⅜″ hole ⅜″ deep directly into the center of the bottom end of each upright, both ends of the top rail, and one end of each armrest. Taper the ends of E, F, and G as shown, then glue the dowel pins (H) into the ⅜″ holes in E, F, and G.

4 For mounting the uprights (E) in the top of the seat, locate and drill ⅜″ holes ⅜″ deep at a compound angle, tilting 5° back and 10° out where shown on the Front and Side View drawings.

5 Drill ⅜″ holes ⅜″ deep into the uprights for the top rail and armrests (the holes for the top rail are drilled at 10° from center while the holes for the armrests are drilled at 5° from center). Drill two holes in the top rail and seat for the back supports (I). Drill a 3/8" hole 1/2" deep in each armrest and seat for the armrest supports (J).

6 Fit the chair together, and redrill as necessary. Glue and clamp the chair together. (We used band clamps on the legs and a variety of clamps on the chair back and armrest assemblies.)

7 Cut the tray arms (K), tray (L), spacers (M), and dowel pins (N) to size. Chamfer the inside end of each spacer (M). Cut a trough in the tray by fitting the router in your router table with a 3/8" diameter core-box bit. Make the outside cuts using the fence to keep the raised edges on each side, then use a straight bit to clean out the center.

8 Glue and clamp the tray (L) between the tray arms (K), drill holes where indicated on the drawing, and dowel the pieces together.

9 Glue one spacer (M) to each tray arm (K). After the glue dries, drill a 3/16" hole through the center of each M and on through the tray arm. Position the tray assembly against the uprights (E), and drill a pilot hole into each upright.

10 Finish-sand the chair and tray assembly. (We found it easier to hand-sand the pieces rather than trying to use a palm sander.) Apply the finish, and screw the tray to the chair with a pair of wood screws.

Continued

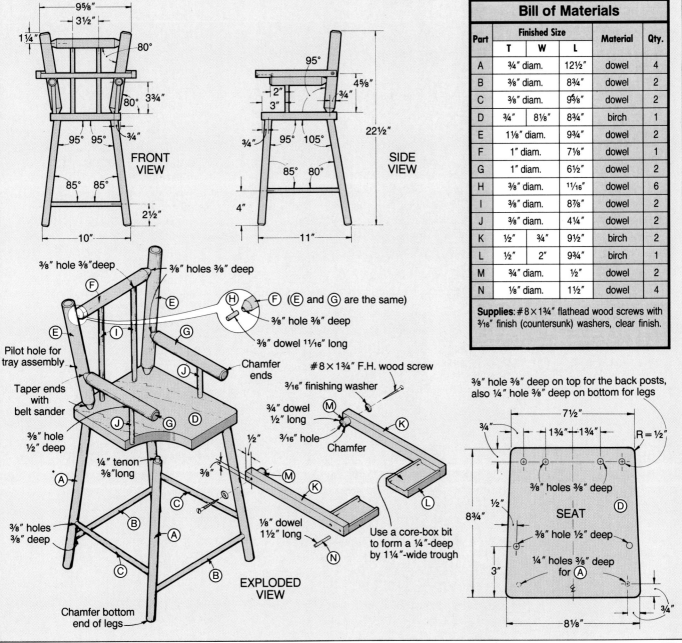

FRONT VIEW

SIDE VIEW

Bill of Materials

Part	Finished Size			Material	Qty.
	T	**W**	**L**		
A	3/4" diam.		12 1/2"	dowel	4
B	3/8" diam.		8 3/4"	dowel	2
C	3/8" diam.		9 5/8"	dowel	2
D	3/4"	8 1/8"	8 3/4"	birch	1
E	1 1/8" diam.		9 3/4"	dowel	2
F	1" diam.		7 1/8"	dowel	1
G	1" diam.		6 1/2"	dowel	2
H	3/8" diam.		11/16"	dowel	6
I	3/8" diam.		8 7/8"	dowel	2
J	3/8" diam.		4 1/4"	dowel	2
K	1/2"	3/4"	9 1/2"	birch	2
L	1/2"	2"	9 3/4"	birch	1
M	3/4" diam.		1/2"	dowel	2
N	1/8" diam.		1 1/2"	dowel	4

Supplies: #8 × 1 3/4" flathead wood screws with 3/16" finish (countersunk) washers, clear finish.

3/8" hole 3/8" deep on top for the back posts, also 1/4" hole 3/8" deep on bottom for legs

SEAT

EXPLODED VIEW

SCHOOLTIME DESK

1 Rip, then miter-cut the eight pieces that make up the desk's legs (A) to size. Now, cut the stretcher (B), the seat support (C), and the dowel pins (D) used to fortify the leg joints, and the desktop (E) to size. Refer to the Parts View drawing when cutting C to shape.

2 Cut a ¼" dado ⅜" deep in the center of two of the leg parts and the stretcher. Cut a tongue on each end of the stretcher, and one on the end of the seat support.

3 Glue and clamp the legs together. Drill ¼" holes 1½" deep at each joint, then glue and install the dowel pins (D). Sand the legs smooth and the dowel pins flush.

4 Route a pencil rest (¼" vein) in the top surface of the desktop

where shown in the Exploded View drawing. Then, glue and clamp the stretcher (B) and the desktop (E) between the legs (see the Side View drawing for how to position the desktop). Drill pilot holes for the screws and plugs to join A to E. Drive the screws, and glue the plugs over the screw heads.

5 Glue the seat support (C) to the stretcher (B). Cut the seat (F), the backrest support (G), and the backrest (H) to shape as dimensioned on the Parts View drawing. Glue and screw the seat to the backrest support (see the Side View drawing).

6 Glue and screw the backrest to the backrest support, using a pair of #8×¾" wood screws covered with ⅜" plugs.

7 Round off sharp edges, sand the desk, and apply the finish. 🌳

Bill of Materials

Part	Finished Size			Material	Qty.
	T	W	L		
A	¾"	1¼"	7"	birch	8
B	¾"	1¼"	10½"	birch	1
C	¾"	2½"	10⅛"	birch	1
D*	¼" diam.		1½"	dowel	8
E	¾"	6"	9¾"	birch	1
F	¾"	6¼"	7½"	birch	1
G	¾"	2"	6¼"	birch	1
H	¾"	2"	6⅜"	birch	1

*This part is cut larger initially, then trimmed to finished size. Please read instructions before cutting.

Supplies: #8×2¼" flathead wood screws, #8×1½" flathead wood screws, #8×¾" flathead wood screws, clear finish.

Project Design: Jim Boelling
Photographs: Hopkins Associates
Illustrations: Bill Zaun, Randall Foshee

PARTS VIEW

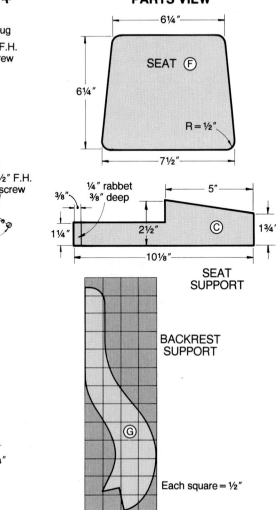

EXPLODED VIEW

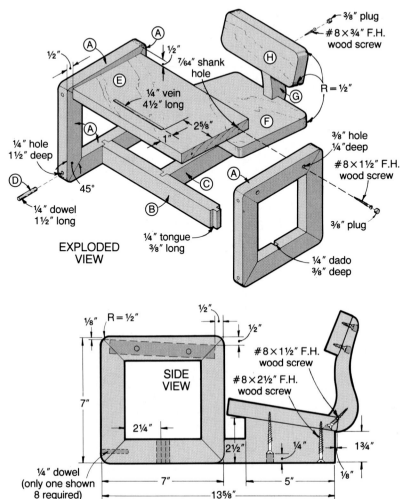

Craig Lossing

TIP-TOP TOPS

GIVE THIS PATTERN A SPIN

Craig Lossing markets at crafts fairs from his lake-dotted home state of Minnesota to sunny Arizona. Although he specializes in bowls, this Minneapolis native quickly notes that few people leave his booth without giving one of his tops a spin. Priced at less than $5 apiece, his top sales often pay more than a third of his exhibit fee.

Although the shapes of his two most popular sellers resemble each other somewhat (see the full-sized patterns at *right*), Craig creates distinctiveness by experimenting with several types of woods. "Domestic woods such as ash, walnut, and maple are lighter and easier for younger hands to spin," Craig notes. "Exotic woods such as cocobolo, bocote, and ebony tend to be heavier, spin longer, and have more dramatic grain."

How Craig mounts and turns the tops

This creative woodturner starts by cutting a piece of stock to 2″ square by 5″ long. (If you don't have stock this thick, laminate thinner stock to size.) Next, he marks diagonals on one end to find center, drills a pilot hole at the centerpoint, and threads the turning square onto a screw center.

With a ½″ gouge—the only tool he needs to fashion the tops—Craig turns the square round. As shown in Step 1 on the three-step drawing at *right*, Craig turns and sands the bottom. Then, as shown in Step 2, he shapes and sands the disc. "It's important to sand after shaping each portion," Craig states. "If you wait until the very end to sand, it's easy to snap the thin handles."

Finally, Craig turns the handle. "Rather than apply tool pressure directly against the handle, I angle the tool and direct some pressure toward the headstock to lessen the chance of breaking the handle," Craig says. Then, he carefully sands the handle and parts the top from the faceplate. Craig finishes his tops with mineral oil.

Taking it out for a spin: it's all in the fingers

"You'll get a longer spin time using your thumb and middle finger rather than your weaker index finger," Craig claims. "Also, with a bit of practice, you can spin these tops on their handles."🌳

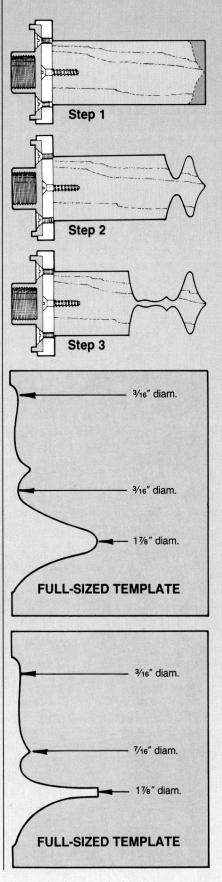

Step 1

Step 2

Step 3

3/16″ diam.

3/16″ diam.

1⅞″ diam.

FULL-SIZED TEMPLATE

3/16″ diam.

7/16″ diam.

1⅞″ diam.

FULL-SIZED TEMPLATE

Another in a collection of patterns from the nation's top woodturners

Photographs:
Jim Kascoutas;
Gail Space
Illustrations:
Kim Downing;
Bill Zaun

Project Design:
Craig Lossing, 1768
Norfolk Ave., St. Paul,
MN 55116

DUNE JUMPIN' BAJA BUGGY

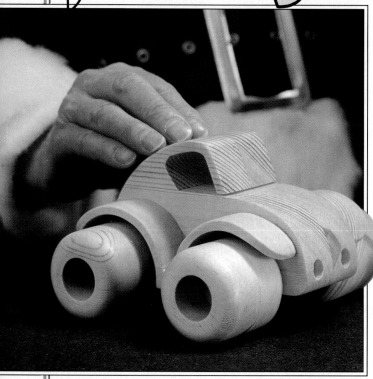

Youngsters will feel the wind through their hair and the summer sun upon their faces when driving this beach buggy over the dunes of make-believe. This fat-tired toy requires just a few feet of 2×4 stock and about 2½ hours to build. Can you think of an easier child pleaser?

Shape the body and fenders

1 Plane or resaw two 12"-long pieces of pine or fir 2×4 stock to 1¹⁄₁₆" thick. You also could use five-quarter (5/4) stock and eliminate the planing. Glue and clamp the pieces together face to face for the car body (A).

2 Transfer the full-sized car outline and axle-hole locations to a piece of paper. (We photocopied the pattern; you also could use carbon paper.) Cut the pattern outline to shape. Apply spray-on adhesive to the back side of the paper pattern, and stick the pattern to the pine block.

3 Drill a pair of ⁷⁄₁₆" axle holes through the body where marked.

4 With a ⅛" blade on your band saw, cut the car body and window opening to shape.

5 Plane or resaw another 12"-long piece of 2×4 stock to 1¹⁄₁₆" thick. Using the same transfer procedure described in step 2, lay out and cut the two fenders (B) to shape.

6 Sand a radius on the front and rear outside corners of the fenders as shown in the Fender Detail. (We marked the radii with a quarter, and shaped the radii with a belt sander.)

7 Remove the paper pattern, and hand-sand the car body and fenders.

8 Drill a pair of ⁷⁄₁₆" holes ¼" deep in the front of the car body to form the headlights. (We held the car body upright in a handscrew clamp, and drilled the holes on the drill press.)

9 Glue and clamp the fenders to the car body where located on the Full-Sized Pattern. The bottom middle section of the fenders should be flush with the bottom of the car body. Wipe off the excess glue with a damp cloth.

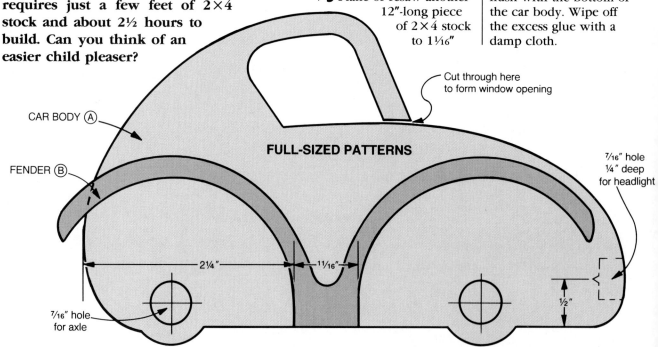

Cut through here to form window opening

CAR BODY (A)

FENDER (B)

FULL-SIZED PATTERNS

⁷⁄₁₆" hole ¼" deep for headlight

2¼"

1¹⁄₁₆"

½"

⁷⁄₁₆" hole for axle

Let's add the wheels

1 Plane two 12″ lengths of 2×4 stock to 1¹⁄₁₆″. Laminate the two pieces together face to face. Allow the glue to dry.

2 Using a compass, mark four 2⅛″-diameter (1¹⁄₁₆″ radius) circles on the top face of the laminated stock for the wheels (C).

3 Chuck a 1″ Forstner or paddle bit into your drill press. Drill a 1¹⁄₁₆″-deep hole at the center of each marked wheel. Switch to a brad-point bit, and drill a ⅜″ hole through the center of each wheel.

4 Using a band saw, cut the four wheels to shape, cutting just outside the marked outline.

5 Fasten a wheel to a 5″-long piece of ⅜″-threaded rod where shown on the drawing at *right.* Chuck the assembly into your drill press. With 80-grit sandpaper, sand the wheels smooth (we used a sanding block). Sand a ⅜″ round-over along the outside edges. With the drill press stopped, check the sanded round-overs for uniformity with a ⅜″ round-over bit as shown at *right.* Finish-sand with finer grits of paper. Repeat the process for the remaining wheels.

6 From ⅜″ dowel stock, cut two axles 4⅜″ long each. Glue one axle, flush with inside edge of the 1″ hole, to each wheel. (See the Exploded-View Drawing for reference.) Insert the axles through the car body, and glue on the other two wheels so the wheel-axle assemblies rotate easily.

Apply the finish and head for the dunes

1 Apply two coats of clear finish. (We found that an oil finish tends to pick up too much dirt over time, but, paint, lacquer, or polyurethane work well.) Now, watch a deserving youngster's imagination run wild.

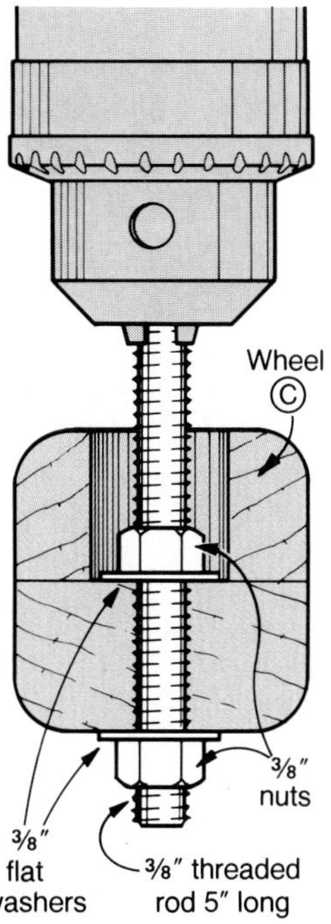

Wheel
C
⅜″ nuts
⅜″ flat washers
⅜″ threaded rod 5″ long

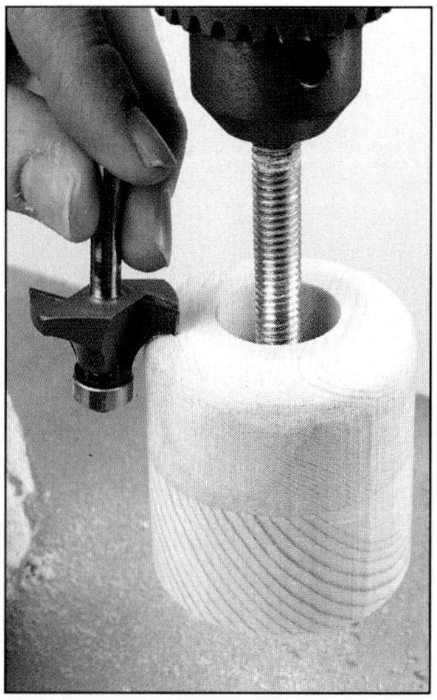

When sanding the band-sawed wheels to shape on the drill press, check round-overs with a ⅜″ round-over bit for uniformity.

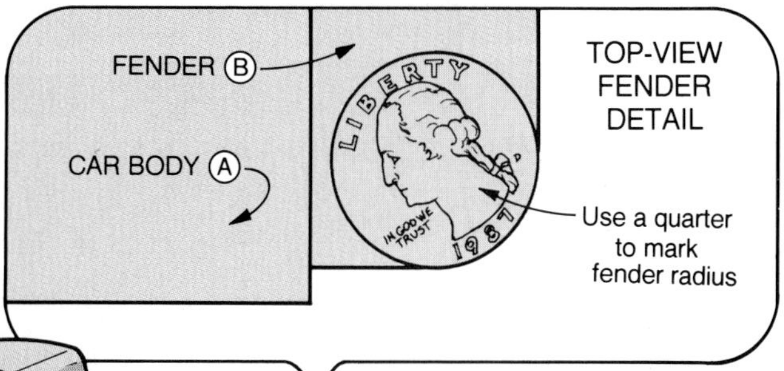

FENDER B
CAR BODY A
TOP-VIEW FENDER DETAIL
Use a quarter to mark fender radius

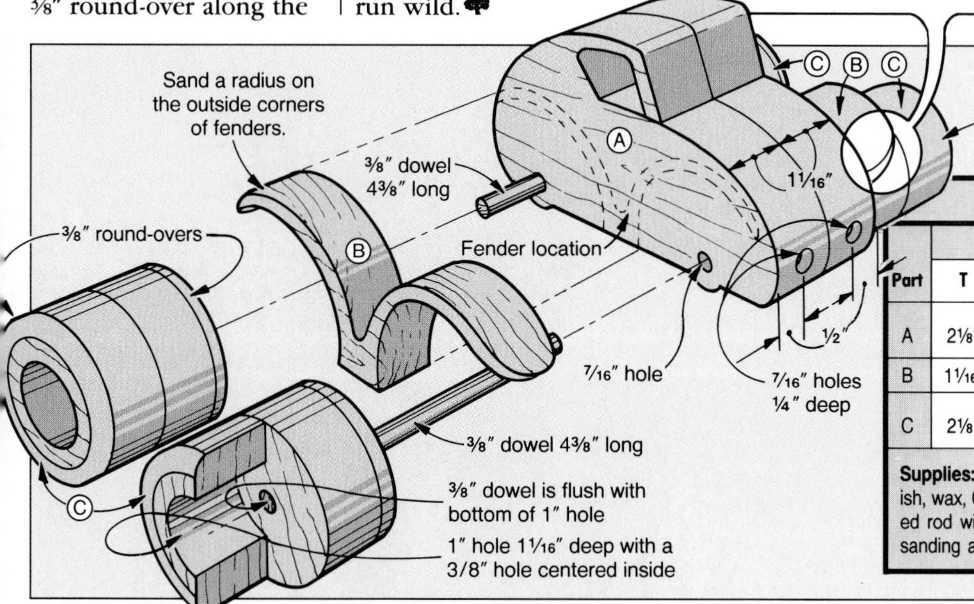

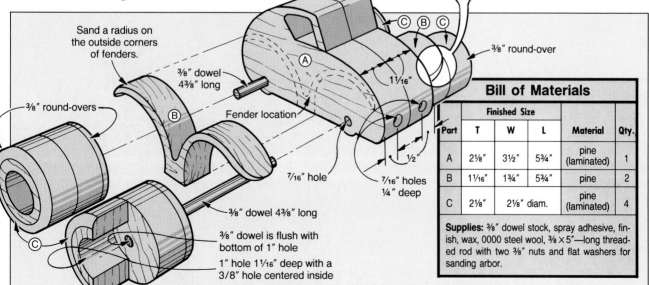

Sand a radius on the outside corners of fenders.
C B C
⅜″ round-over
A
⅜″ dowel 4⅜″ long
1¹⁄₁₆″
⅜″ round-overs
B
Fender location
½″
7⁄16″ hole
7⁄16″ holes ¼″ deep
⅜″ dowel 4⅜″ long
C
⅜″ dowel is flush with bottom of 1″ hole
1″ hole 1¹⁄₁₆″ deep with a 3/8″ hole centered inside

Bill of Materials

Part	Finished Size			Material	Qty.
	T	W	L		
A	2⅛″	3½″	5¾″	pine (laminated)	1
B	1¹⁄₁₆″	1¾″	5¾″	pine	2
C	2⅛″	2⅛″ diam.		pine (laminated)	4

Supplies: ⅜″ dowel stock, spray adhesive, finish, wax, 0000 steel wool, ⅜ × 5″—long threaded rod with two ⅜″ nuts and flat washers for sanding arbor.

Project Design: James R. Downing Photographs: Jim Kascoutas Illustrations: Kim Downing; Mike Henry

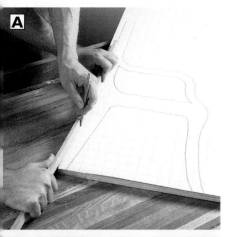

Tea for Two!

Tiny Table and Chairs

Jill and Bailey, two very proper 4-year-olds, shared afternoon tea at *WOOD* Magazine not long ago. Our little table and chairs helped the occasion seem very grown-up indeed. Build this set from just one 4x8′ sheet of plywood (we used ribbon-stripe mahogany) and delight someone special.

First, cut out the chairs

1 Cut your plywood panel into two 48×48″ pieces. Noting the direction of the veneer grain in the Cutting Diagram, page 80, rip two 13×48″ pieces from one of the pieces to yield four chair sides (A).

2 Using a ruler and a straightedge, lay out 1″ squares on a large piece of heavy paper to form a 15×30″ grid pattern. Transfer the profile of the chair side from the Chair Grid drawing, *below*, to the full-sized pattern. (To form the long curve on the back leg, we worked with a helper and bent a flexible strip of wood as shown in photo A, *left*.)

3 Use spray adhesive or double-faced tape to secure the pattern to the plywood. Use a bandsaw or

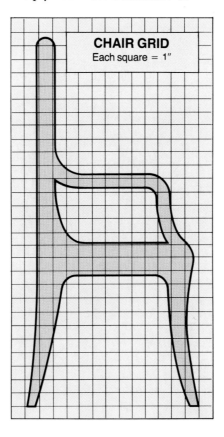

CHAIR GRID
Each square = 1″

jigsaw fitted with a fine-toothed blade to cut the chair side to shape, cutting just *outside* the marked lines. To make the cutouts, drill a blade-access hole through the chair side, then cut just *inside* the marked line with a jigsaw.

4 Sand the chair side to finished shape. (This side will serve as a template for the others, so take your time.) Now, remove the pattern, and sand off any sticky residue.

5 Trace the outline of your chair-side template onto the ¾″ plywood for the three remaining chair sides. Cut the chair sides to shape, cutting slightly to the scrap side of the marked lines.

6 Use double-faced tape to stick the template to one of the rough-cut chair sides. Center the template on the rough-cut piece so that the excess of the rough-cut piece protrudes over both edges of the template. Then, fit your router with a ¼″ flush-trim bit. With the template on the bottom, lower the bit so that the pilot rides on the template, and trim the rough-cut side to shape as shown in photo B, *far left*. Now, separate the two chair sides, and repeat the routing procedure with the remaining sides, always using the same template. Sand the routed edges smooth.

7 Lay out the shape of the backrest (B) on a piece of paper (see the Front View drawing, page 80, for dimensions). Cut the pattern and secure it to the plywood as shown in photo C, *far left*. Trace the outline of the backrest onto the plywood, and remove the pattern. Drill ½″ blade-access holes where necessary for the interior cuts, and cut the backrest to shape with a

Continued

Tiny Table and Chairs

scrollsaw or jigsaw. Finally, sand all the edges smooth.

8 Using the first backrest as a template, make the second, just as you made the second chair side (refer back to steps 5 and 6).

Assembling the chairs

1 Cut the stretchers (C) to the size listed in the Bill of Materials. Locate the center of each rail end, and drill a ⅛" pilot hole ½" deep for later ease in fastening between the chair

sides. Sand a slight round-over on the bottom edges of each stretcher.

2 Mark the location of the stretcher and backrest mounting-screw holes on one chair side where indicated on the Exploded View drawing. Stack the chair sides in pairs, and drill ⁵⁄₃₂" pilot holes through both sides where marked. Switch to a ⅜" drill bit and counterbore the holes ⅜" deep on the outside face of each chair side.

3 Dry-clamp the chair sides, stretchers, and backrest together, tilting the backrest where shown in the Side Section drawing, *below*. (We used a small nail to help line up the holes in the stretchers with the holes in the chair sides.) Drive the screws into place. Switch back to a ⅛" bit and drill the mounting holes ½" deep into the backrest, centered through the ⁵⁄₃₂" holes drilled in the previous step.

Cutting Diagram (TWO CHAIRS)

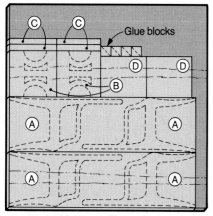

¾ x 48 x 48" Mahogany Plywood

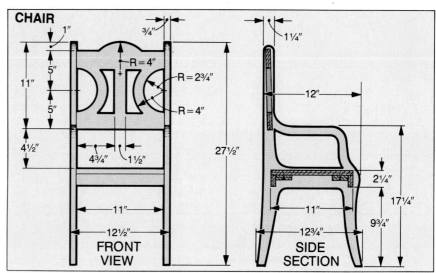

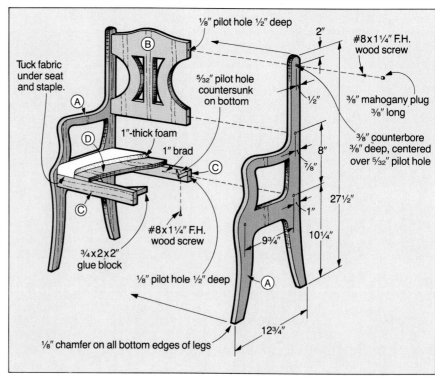

Bill of Materials

	(FOR TWO CHAIRS)				
Part	Finished Size*			Material	Qty.
	T	W	L		
A*	¾"	12¾"	27½"	mahogany plywood	4
B	¾"	11"	11"	mahogany plywood	2
C	¾"	1½"	11"	mahogany plywood	4
D	¾"	11"	10⅞"	mahogany plywood	2

*Parts marked with a * are cut larger initially, then trimmed to finished size. Please read the instructions before cutting.

Supplies: #8x1¼" flathead wood screws, #8x1" flathead wood screws, 1" wire brads, wood filler, polyurethane-sanding sealer, stain, polyurethane, paste wax, #0000 steel wool, double-faced tape, heavy paper for grid patterns, 1" foam padding, 1 sq. yd. upholstery fabric

4 Back out the #8 × 1¼″ rail mounting screws and apply glue to the stretcher and backrest ends. With the chair on a flat surface, screw the stretchers and backrest in position, checking the stretchers and backrest for square against the chair sides.

5 Using a ⅜″ plug cutter, cut 16 plugs from solid mahogany stock planed down to ⁷⁄₁₆″. Glue a plug in place over each of the screws, matching the direction of the grain with the chair sides. When the glue dries, sand the plugs flush, being careful not to sand through the plywood veneer.

6 Cut the triangular glue blocks to the size indicated on the Exploded View drawing. Then, use glue and 1″ brads to attach them to the chair frame flush with the top edges of the stretchers. Drill and countersink a ⁵⁄₃₂″ mounting hole on the bottom of the glue block.

7 Cut the chair seat (D) to the size listed in the Bill of Materials. (The seat measures ⅛″ narrower than the completed chair frame to allow for the upholstery.) Then, use the seat as a template to cut a pad from 1″-thick foam. Now, cut two pieces of upholstery to 17×17″, and staple the upholstery as shown in photo D, *below.*

8 Position the seat where shown in the Side Section drawing. Drill ⅛″ pilot holes ½″ deep, using the previously drilled holes in the glue blocks as guides.

Constructing the table

1 Cut two 22×19¼″ plywood pieces for the table legs (E) as shown in the Cutting Diagram.

2 As you did with the chairs, lay out on paper a 1″ grid pattern measuring 21×24″. Mark the vertical centerline. Working from the right side of the centerline, transfer the half shape of the table leg to the grid (see drawing, *below*).

3 Fold the grid paper along the centerline, and tape the top and bottom edges of the halves togeth-

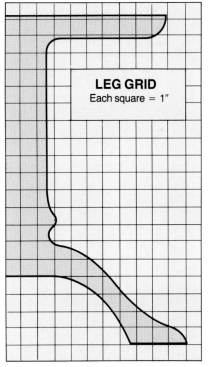

LEG GRID
Each square = 1″

er. Cut out the pattern, remove the tape, and unfold the paper to yield a full-sized leg pattern.

4 Tape or use spray adhesive to secure the pattern in place, then trace the leg outline onto the plywood. Use a jigsaw to cut the leg to shape, cutting just *outside* the outline. Sand the edges smooth.

5 Using the first leg as a template, follow the procedure in steps 5 and 6, page 79, to form the second leg.

6 Lay out and mark a ¾″ notch 7⅝″ long on each of the legs where shown on the Exploded View drawing on the next page. Cut the notches with a scrollsaw fitted with a fine-toothed blade. Sand the edges of the notches. (We wrapped sandpaper around a flat scrap of wood to keep the notches straight when sanding.) Glue and clamp the assembly, checking for square.

7 Cut a piece of ¾″ plywood to 28½×28½″ for the tabletop (F). Place the top with the best face down on a clean work surface, being careful not to scratch the veneer face. Mark diagonal lines from opposite corners of the top to locate the center. Drill a ¼″ hole ½″ deep at the centerpoint, taking care not to drill through the tabletop (we used a stop on our drill bit to prevent drilling too deep).

8 From ¼″ hardboard, construct a trammel base like the one shown and described in the drawing, *below,* for your router.

Continued

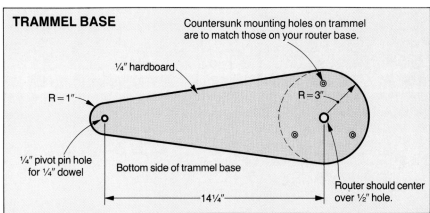

TRAMMEL BASE
Countersunk mounting holes on trammel are to match those on your router base.
¼″ hardboard
R = 1″
R = 3″
¼″ pivot pin hole for ¼″ dowel
Bottom side of trammel base
14¼″
Router should center over ½″ hole.

Tiny Table and Chairs

Bill of Materials

Part	Finished Size*			Material	Qty.
	T	W	L		
E*	¾"	22"	19¼"	mahogany plywood	2
F*	¾"	28" diam.		mahogany plywood	1

*Parts marked with a * are cut larger initially, then trimmed to finished size. Please read the instructions before cutting.

Supplies: #8x2″ flathead wood screws, ¼″ dowel, same finishing supplies as chairs .

Cutting Diagram (TABLE)

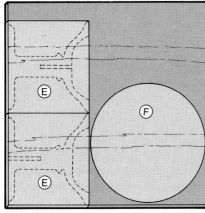

E

F

E

¾ x 48 x 48″ Mahogany Plywood

E

TABLE

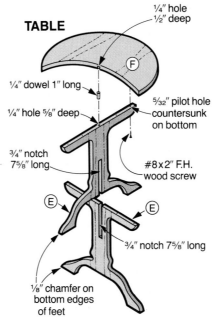

¼" hole ½" deep

F

¼" dowel 1" long

¼" hole ⅝" deep

⁵⁄₃₂" pilot hole countersunk on bottom

¾" notch 7⅝" long

#8×2" F.H. wood screw

E   E

¾" notch 7⅝" long

⅛" chamfer on bottom edges of feet

9 Mount the trammel base on a ¼" dowel pin in the centered hole in the bottom of the tabletop. With a ½" straight bit, slowly rout the round tabletop as shown in photo E, *left*. Set the router to cut ¼" deep initially, followed by successively deeper passes (place a scrap piece of plywood below the tabletop blank to protect your workbench surface on the final pass).

10 Drill a ¼" hole ⅝" deep centered in the top of the leg assembly, then glue a ¼" dowel 1" long in the hole. Glue and clamp the top in place. With a ⁵⁄₃₂" bit, drill, then countersink two holes in each leg where shown on the Exploded View drawing. Further secure the tabletop to the leg assembly with #8×2" wood screws.

The perfect finish

1 Fill any voids or chips in the veneer with wood filler (we used mahogany-colored Fix Wood Patch). Finish-sand the chair frames and the table (we started with 150-grit and finished off with 220-grit sandpaper). Then, sand a very slight sandpaper break on all edges to prevent splintering. Using a sanding block, sand a ⅛" chamfer on the bottom edges of each chair leg and the feet of the table to prevent snagging carpets and rugs.

2 Stain the pieces. Apply two coats of polyurethane-sanding sealer, rubbing between coats with 220-grit abrasive.

3 Apply several coats of clear polyurethane, sanding lightly between coats. When the last coat has dried, rub the pieces with 0000 steel wool and paste wax. Put a final buff on the finish with a soft cloth. (We found that a piece of terry-cloth mounted on a palm sander worked great.)

4 Screw the upholstered seats in place, and deliver the furniture to its new owner. 🌳

Produced by Marlen Kemmet
  with Kerry Gibson
Photographs: Jim Kascoutas
Illustrations: Kim Downing

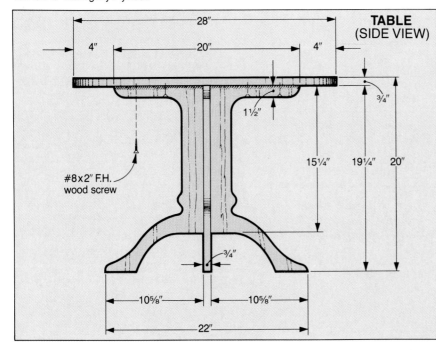

TABLE (SIDE VIEW)

28"

4"   20"   4"

¾"

#8×2" F.H. wood screw

1½"

15¼"   19¼"   20"

¾"

10⅝"   10⅝"

22"

4-PACK OF CARS

1 Cut part A to size from a 2×8. Round off all the sharp edges and corners, then sand smooth.

2 Transfer the design to the stock. Locate all axle centerpoints, windows, and cut lines.

3 Drill 5⁄16″ axle holes and 1⁄2″ window holes where marked.

4 Cut out the cars, using a bandsaw with a 1⁄8″ blade.

5 Transfer the pattern for the handle (B) onto a piece of contrasting stock and cut it out. Round off the handle edges with a rasp. Sand the cars and the handle.

6 Add interest to the cars by making the 1¼″ wheels (C) from a contrasting wood. Using a 1½″ holesaw, cut through the stock until the 1⁄4″ pilot bit of the holesaw penetrates the opposite side of the stock. Remove the holesaw, then flip the stock over and finish the cut.

7 Glue and clamp the carrying case back together at the entry cut. After the glue has set up, remove the clamp, then drill and peg the cut line with a 1⁄4″ dowel. Glue and clamp the handle to the case, and drill 1⁄4″ dowel mounting holes. Add a few drops of glue into each dowel hole, and glue the handle in place. When dry, sand all protruding dowels flush.

8 Drill 1⁄4″ holes in the case. Insert cars and mark for catches, then drill 3⁄8″ holes in the bottom of the cars to accept the catches. Partially plug the holes in the case to the point shown with 1⁄4″ dowels.

9 Insert the axles (D), glue the wheels to the axles, and sand them flush after the glue has dried. Apply a nontoxic finish. Insert the bullet catches. ♣

Design: Steve Baldwin
Photograph: George Ceolla

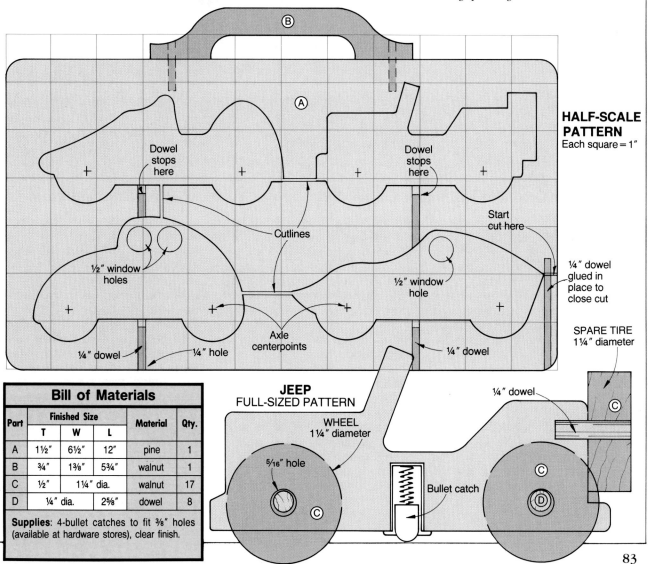

HALF-SCALE PATTERN
Each square = 1″

Dowel stops here

Dowel stops here

Start cut here

Cutlines

1⁄2″ window holes

1⁄2″ window hole

1⁄4″ dowel glued in place to close cut

SPARE TIRE 1¼″ diameter

Axle centerpoints

1⁄4″ dowel

1⁄4″ hole

1⁄4″ dowel

JEEP FULL-SIZED PATTERN

1⁄4″ dowel

WHEEL 1¼″ diameter

5⁄16″ hole

Bullet catch

Bill of Materials

Part	Finished Size			Material	Qty.
	T	W	L		
A	1½″	6½″	12″	pine	1
B	3⁄4″	1⅜″	5¾″	walnut	1
C	1⁄2″	1¼″ dia.		walnut	17
D	1⁄4″ dia.		2⅝″	dowel	8

Supplies: 4-bullet catches to fit 3⁄8″ holes (available at hardware stores), clear finish.

RUBBER-BAND POWERED DRAGSTER

Watch the gleam in your child's eye when this snappy little dragster zips across the floor. Our full-sized pattern makes it easy to build from scrap lumber. Just a few turns of the rear wheels wind it up for the green light.

1 From ½" stock (we used maple), cut a piece 2×6" for the chassis (A). Using carbon paper, transfer the full-sized chassis pattern *at right* onto the stock. Mark the location of the front and rear axle holes, and the centerpoints for the flag and motor pin. Using a drill press and a ⁹⁄₃₂" bit, drill the front and rear axle holes square with the chassis. Switch to a ¼" bit and drill the flag and motor pin holes 15° from vertical. (We simply "eyeballed" the angles when drilling.) Cut the chassis to shape and finish-sand.

2 To make the "slicks" (B), cut two pieces of ½" maple to 3×10". Laminate the pieces together face-to-face. Using a drill press and a 2" holesaw or circle cutter, cut

out the two rear wheels. Switch to a 1" holesaw, and cut two front wheels (C) from ⅝" stock.

3 Mount a length of ¼" dowel in the drill press, and slide a wheel onto the dowel. Start the drill press, and sand the wheel smooth, putting a slight round-over on the edges. Repeat the process for the other three wheels.

4 From ¼" dowel stock, cut the front and rear axles, flagstaff, and motor pin to the lengths indicated on the Exploded View drawing. Drill a ¹⁄₃₂" hole ³⁄₁₆" deep in the center of the rear axle.

5 Glue one rear wheel onto the rear axle and one front wheel onto the front axle. Insert the axles through the body. Then, glue the other wheels to the appropri

ate axles, and glue the motor pin and flagstaff in place.

6 Grind the tip of a #4 finish nail until it measures ⅝" long. Apply a small amount of epoxy to the tip of the nail; then gently tap it into the hole in the rear axle.

7 Cut a 4" strip of ¾" wide colored plastic tape for the flag, wrap around the flagstaff, and cut it to shape. Attach the rubber bands for the "ties" and the "motor." To "fuel" the dragster, wind the rear wheels, holding the wheels between strokes to prevent them from spinning. Still holding the wheels, set the car on a smooth surface, and "let 'er rip." 🌳

Project Design: Michael Spikes
Photograph: Bob Calmer
Illustrations: Kim Downing; Bill Zaun

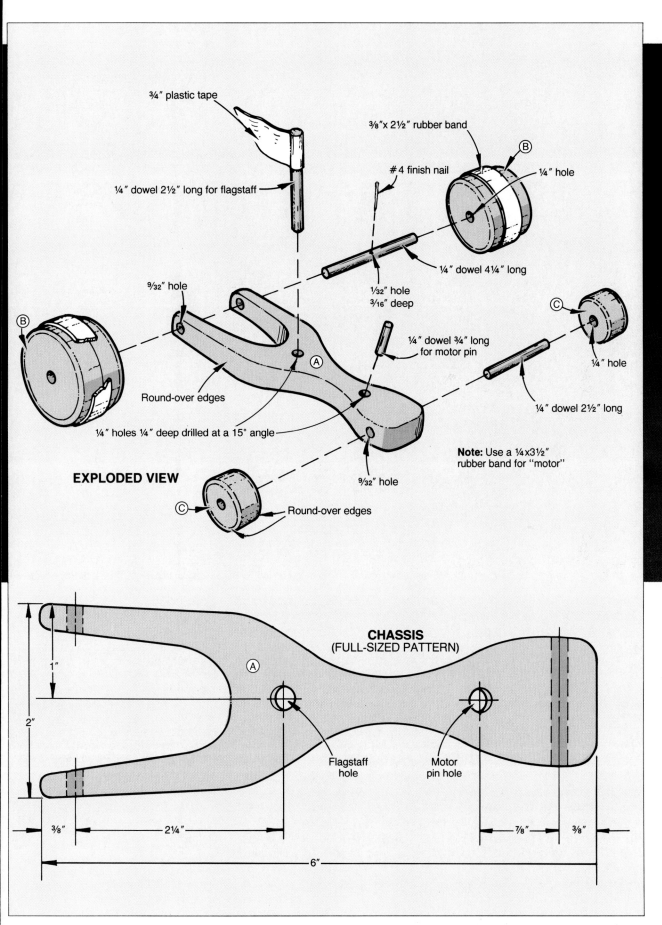

¾″ plastic tape

¼″ dowel 2½″ long for flagstaff

⅜″ x 2½″ rubber band

4 finish nail

¼″ hole

B

¼″ dowel 4¼″ long

¹⁄₃₂″ hole
³⁄₁₆″ deep

⁹⁄₃₂″ hole

B

¼″ dowel ¾″ long
for motor pin

C

¼″ hole

Round-over edges

¼″ dowel 2½″ long

A

¼″ holes ¼″ deep drilled at a 15° angle

Note: Use a ¼x3½″
rubber band for "motor"

EXPLODED VIEW

⁹⁄₃₂″ hole

C

Round-over edges

CHASSIS
(FULL-SIZED PATTERN)

A

1″

2″

Flagstaff
hole

Motor
pin hole

⅜″

2¼″

⅞″

⅜″

6″

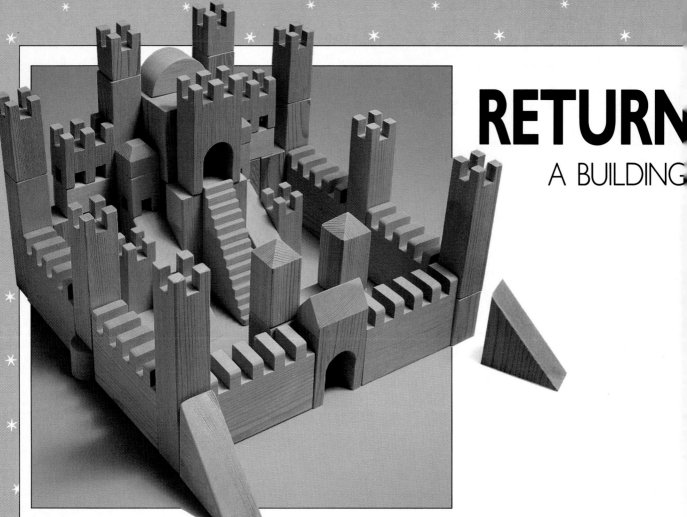

What better way to unleash your little prince or princess's active imagination then with this castle? Look close when they're done, because the next fortress built is sure to be different. You might want to consider build several; the pieces are a cinch to machine, and the whole castle can be built in an evening.

Note: We cut all the castle pieces from 2×4 and 2×6 clear-heart redwood. Pine or fir also would work.

Let's cut some parts to get this kingdom off the ground

I Cut parts A, B, and C to the sizes listed in the Bill of Materials. Using the Parts View Drawing for reference, mark a 1½" radius with a compass, centered along the bottom edge of part C. Bandsaw the radiused opening to shape, and save the cutout.

2 Cut a piece of 1½"-thick stock to 3½ × 3½". Mark a diagonal from one corner to another, and bandsaw the block into two triangles for parts D. Repeat the process with a 3½ × 5¼" block for parts E.

3 Cut part F to size. Lay out the radiused opening, bandsaw it to shape, and save the cutout. Mark the angled roof lines and bandsaw them to shape.

Less than a knight needed to dado the notches and grooves

I Cut parts G, H, I, and J to the sizes listed in the Bill of Materials. Cut parts K and L to the thickness and width listed plus 3" in length. Parts K and L are cut extra long for safety when cutting the dadoes in the next step.

2 Attach a wooden fence to your miter gauge and a ½" dado blade to your tablesaw. Cut the ¾"-deep dadoes in parts G through L where shown on the Parts View Drawing and as shown in the photo *below.* (We used a stop block to position and support the pieces when making the cuts.)

Clamp the castle piece to an auxiliary fence fastened to your miter gauge when cutting the dadoes.

O THE ROUND TABLE

LOCK CASTLE FOR YOUR LITTLE PRINCE OR PRINCESS

Angle-cut the ends of a 12″ length of 1½″ square stock to form the pointed ends on each part P. For safety, we started with an extra-long piece.

Bill of Materials

Part	Finished Size*			Material	Qty.
	T	W	L		
A	1½″	3½″	5″	redwood	4
B	1½″	3½″	3½″	redwood	4
C	1½″	3½″	5″	redwood	1
D*	1½″	3½″	3½″	redwood	2
E*	1½″	3½″	5¼″	redwood	2
F	1½″	2½″	5″	redwood	1
G	1½″	3½″	5″	redwood	6
H	1½″	2½″	5″	redwood	1
I	1½″	2½″	2½″	redwood	2
J	1½″	1½″	6″	redwood	4
K*	1½″	1½″	3½″	redwood	4
L*	1½″	1½″	2″	redwood	4
M	1½″	1½″	6″	redwood	4
N	1½″	1½″	3½″	redwood	6
O	1½″	1½″	2½″	redwood	4
P*	1½″	1½″	3½″	redwood	2
Q*	1½″	1½″	1¼″	redwood	2
R*	1½″	3½″	3½″	redwood	1
S*	1½″	3½″	5¼″	redwood	1

*Initially cut parts marked with an * oversized. Then, trim each to finished size according to the how-to instructions.

3 Cut ½″ dadoes ¾″ deep, centered in the ends of parts H through L, as shown *below*. Crosscut parts K and L to the length listed in the Bill of Materials.

4 Using a compass, mark the radius and cut the opening in part H to shape. Save the cutout.

Determine the location, and clamp a stop block to your miter-gauge fence to position and support the castle pieces when machining the centered dado.

Cut a few more parts, and let the fun begin

1 Cut parts M, N, and O to size.

2 To form the pointed ends on parts P, start by cutting a piece 1½″ square by 12″ long. Then, tilt your tablesaw blade 45° from vertical. Using your miter gauge with a stop block clamped in place, cut the pointed ends on each end of the 12″-long piece as shown in the photo *above*. Crosscut two Ps to length from the 12″-long piece.

3 For parts Q, cut a piece of 1½″-square stock to 6″ long. Bevel-cut both ends to the shape shown on the Parts View Drawing. Trim one part Q from each end of the 6″-long piece.

4 To make the staircases (R, S), crosscut a 2×4 to 12″ long. Using a combination square, mark ¼ × ¼″ steps on part R and ¼ × ⅜″ steps on part S where shown on the Parts View Drawing. Bandsaw each to shape.

5 Sand all the pieces (we used a palm sander and sanded each piece with 100- and 150-grit paper, forming a slight round-over on all edges). Use a drum sander for the radiused openings. If desired, apply a finish (we left ours unstained and unfinished).

Produced by Marlen Kemmet
Project Design: Donald "Sandy" McNab,
    McNab Puzzles/Designs, Sanger, Calif.
Photographs: Hopkins Associates;
    John Hetherington
Illustrations: Kim Downing; Bill Zaun

Continued

BUILDING-BLOCK CASTLE

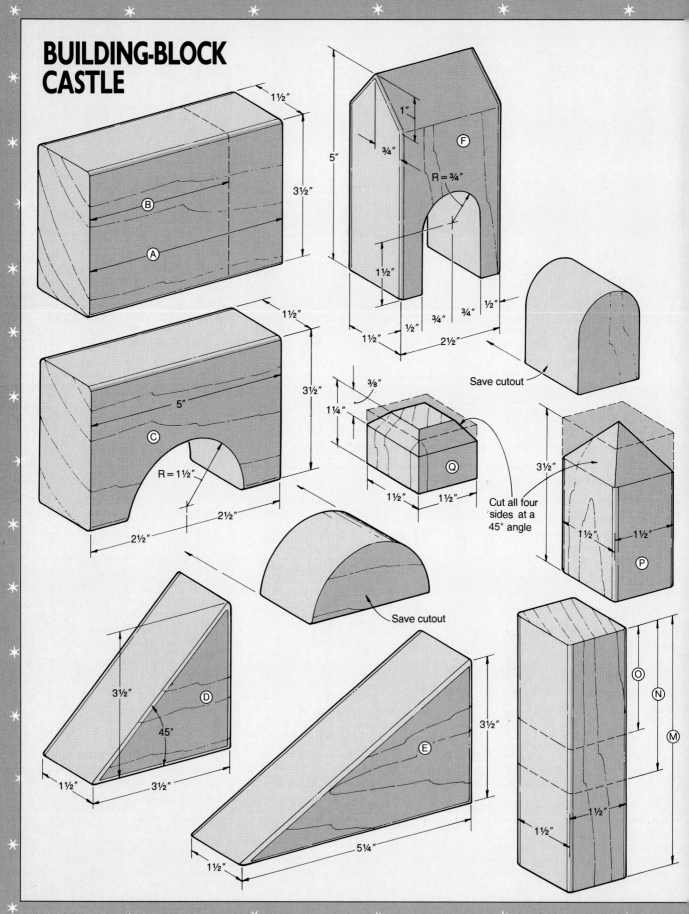

1½"

3½"

B

A

5"

¾"

1"

R = ¾"

F

1½"

½"

½"

¾"

¾"

½"

1½"

2½"

Save cutout

1½"

3½"

5"

C

R = 1½"

2½"

2½"

3/8"

1¼"

Q

1½"

1½"

Cut all four sides at a 45° angle

3½"

1½"

1½"

P

Save cutout

3½"

D

45°

1½"

3½"

3½"

E

5¼"

1½"

O

N

M

1½"

1½"

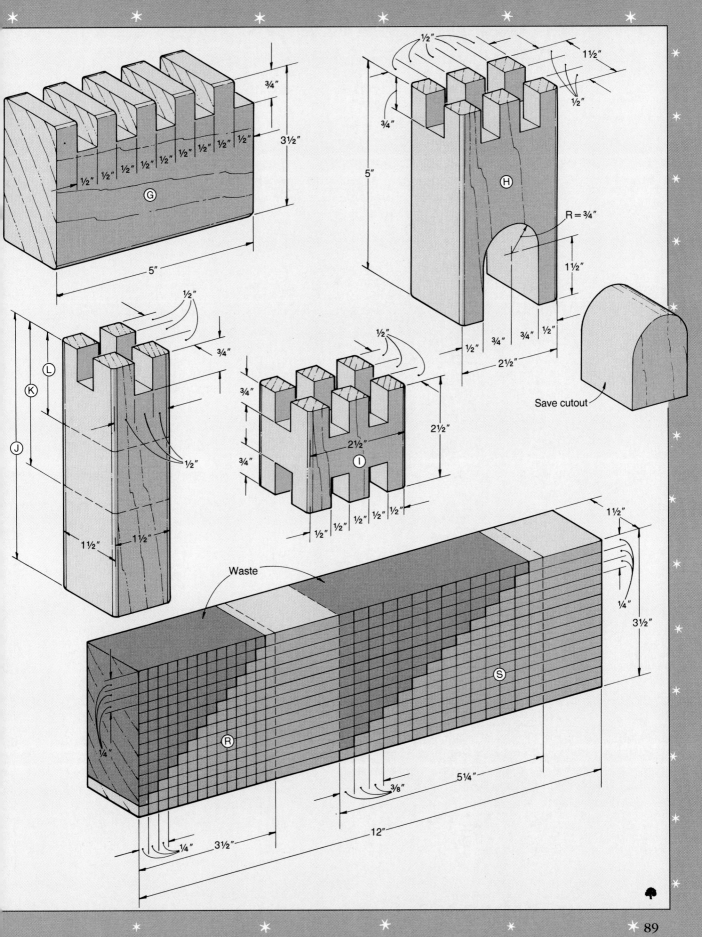

3/4"

3 1/2"

1/2"

1/2" 1/2" 1/2" 1/2" 1/2" 1/2" 1/2" 1/2"

G

5"

1/2"

1 1/2"

1/2"

3/4"

5"

H

R = 3/4"

1 1/2"

1/2" 3/4" 3/4" 1/2"

2 1/2"

Save cutout

1/2"

3/4"

L

K

J

1/2"

1 1/2" 1 1/2"

1/2"

3/4"

3/4"

2 1/2"

2 1/2"

I

1/2" 1/2" 1/2" 1/2" 1/2"

Waste

1 1/2"

1/4"

3 1/2"

S

R

1/4"

3/8"

5 1/4"

1/4"

3 1/2"

12"

THE MIGHTY
TUG·A·LUG

1 From ¾"-thick pine stock, cut the hull sections (A, B) and gunwale (C) to the sizes listed in the Bill of Materials plus ½" in length and width. Using a photocopy and spray adhesive or carbon paper, transfer the full-sized patterns for A, B, and C (shown below) to the pine stock.

2 With a bandsaw or scrollsaw, cut parts A, B, and C to shape, cutting just outside the marked line. Finish-sand the stern (rear section) of A and B, and the inside of the gunwale (C).

3 To distribute the weight evenly and ensure that the tug will float level, bore 2" holes ½" deep and 2" apart on the *top* of hull section A and the *bottom* of the hull section B. Then, bore out the remaining wood between the two holes, and smooth out the rough edges with a chisel to form mirror-image cavities in A and B. Now, bore two 1¼" holes through the top of B into the cavity for the pilothouse (D) and smokestack (E).

4 Drill two ⅝" holes ⅝" deep in the bottom of A to house the four ⁵⁄₁₆" nuts used as ballast. Space the holes 1" apart so you won't hit the nuts when you drill the hole for the bollard. Test-fit the nuts in the holes, and epoxy them in place.

Position the smokestack and pilothouse in a 1¼" hole in a scrap piece of wood. Hold the pieces with handscrew clamps when boring the 1" holes in the center of each with a flat-bottomed bit.

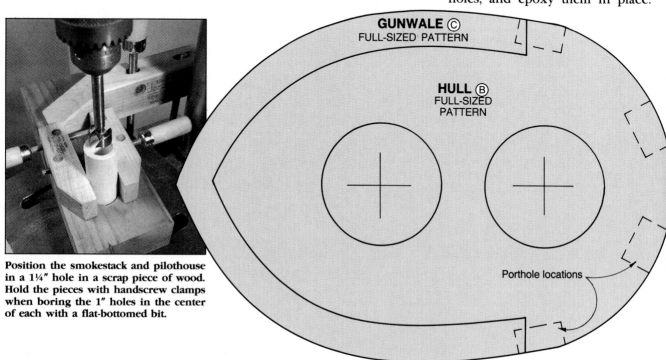

GUNWALE Ⓒ
FULL-SIZED PATTERN

HULL Ⓑ
FULL-SIZED PATTERN

Porthole locations

Next, drill a 3/8″ hole 1/4″ deep in the stern of the A deck to house the bollard (I).

5 Mark the location of the four portholes on the stern of the hull (B). Clamp B in a vise or in a handscrew clamp and drill 3/8″ portholes 1/8″ deep. Using slow-set epoxy, which is waterproof, glue and clamp A, B, and C together.

6 With a belt sander, sand the bow (front end) of the tug to 15° as shown in the Side View drawing *below*, contour-sand the sides, and sand the gunwale (C) so that it tapers from 3/4″ thick in the front to 3/8″ in the back.

7 Cut the pilothouse (D) and smokestack (E) to size from 1 1/4″ dowel stock. Using a wooden V-block to keep the pilothouse dowel in position, drill a 3/4″ hole 5/8″ down from the top end of the dowel for the windows. Now, fashion a smokestack drilling jig like the one shown in the how-to photo. Use the jig to centerbore a 1″ hole 2 1/2″ deep in the smokestack, and a 1″ hole 1 7/8″ deep in the pilothouse.

8 Glue and install the pilothouse and smokestack 1/4″ into deck (B).

9 Cut the roof (F) and the whistle pieces (G, H) to size. Cut the bollard (I) to size plus 1″, and cut

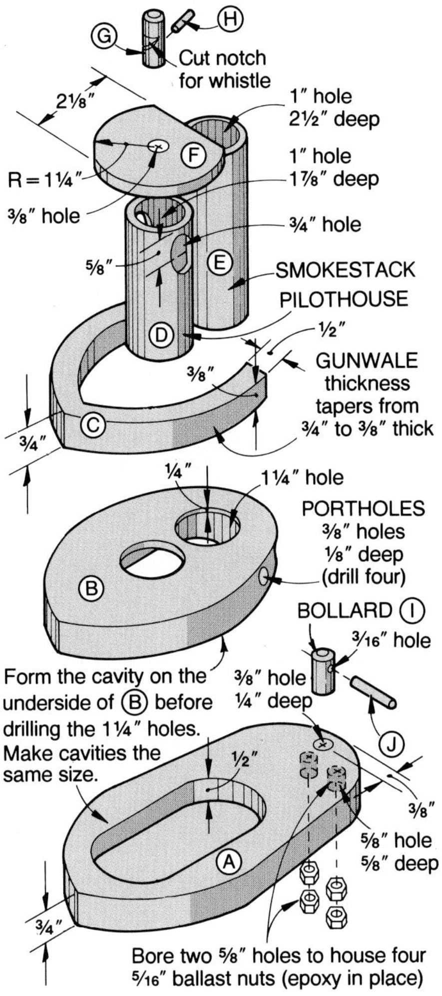

G
H
Cut notch for whistle
2 1/8″
1″ hole 2 1/2″ deep
R = 1 1/4″
F
1″ hole 1 7/8″ deep
3/8″ hole
3/4″ hole
5/8″
E
SMOKESTACK
PILOTHOUSE
D
1/2″
GUNWALE thickness tapers from 3/4″ to 3/8″ thick
3/8″
C
3/4″
1/4″
1 1/4″ hole
PORTHOLES 3/8″ holes 1/8″ deep (drill four)
B
BOLLARD I
3/16″ hole
Form the cavity on the underside of B before drilling the 1 1/4″ holes. Make cavities the same size.
3/8″ hole 1/4″ deep
J
1/2″
3/8″
5/8″ hole 5/8″ deep
A
3/4″
Bore two 5/8″ holes to house four 5/16″ ballast nuts (epoxy in place)

Bill of Materials

Part	Finished Size*			Material	Qty.
	T	W	L		
A*	3/4″	3 1/2″	6 1/2″	pine	1
B*	3/4″	3 1/2″	5 1/4″	pine	1
C*	3/4″	3 1/2″	3 3/4″	pine	1
D	1 1/4″ dia.		2 1/8″	birch dwl.	1
E	1 1/4″ dia.		2 3/4″	birch dwl.	1
F*	1/4″	2 1/2″	2 1/8″	pine	1
G	3/8″ diam.		1″	birch dwl.	1
H	1/8″ diam.		5/8″	birch dwl.	1
I*	3/8″ diam.		1 1/4″	birch dwl.	1
J	3/16″ diam.		1″	birch dwl.	1

*Initially cut parts marked with an * oversized. Then, trim each to finished size according to the how-to instructions.

Supplies: epoxy, exterior polyurethane, 4 - 5/16″ nuts (for ballast)

J to size. Drill a 3/8″ hole through the center of the roof for the whistle. Cut the notch with a fine-toothed saw and chamfer the top end of whistle piece G. Drill a 1/8″ hole for H in G at a 45° angle, and glue H in place. Now, glue the whistle to the roof, and the roof to the pilothouse.

10 Drill a 3/16″ hole through the bollard (I). Chamfer the top end of I and glue J in place.

11 Finish-sand and apply several coats of exterior polyurethane.

Design: Jim Downing
Photograph: Hopkins Associates
Illustration: Mike Henry

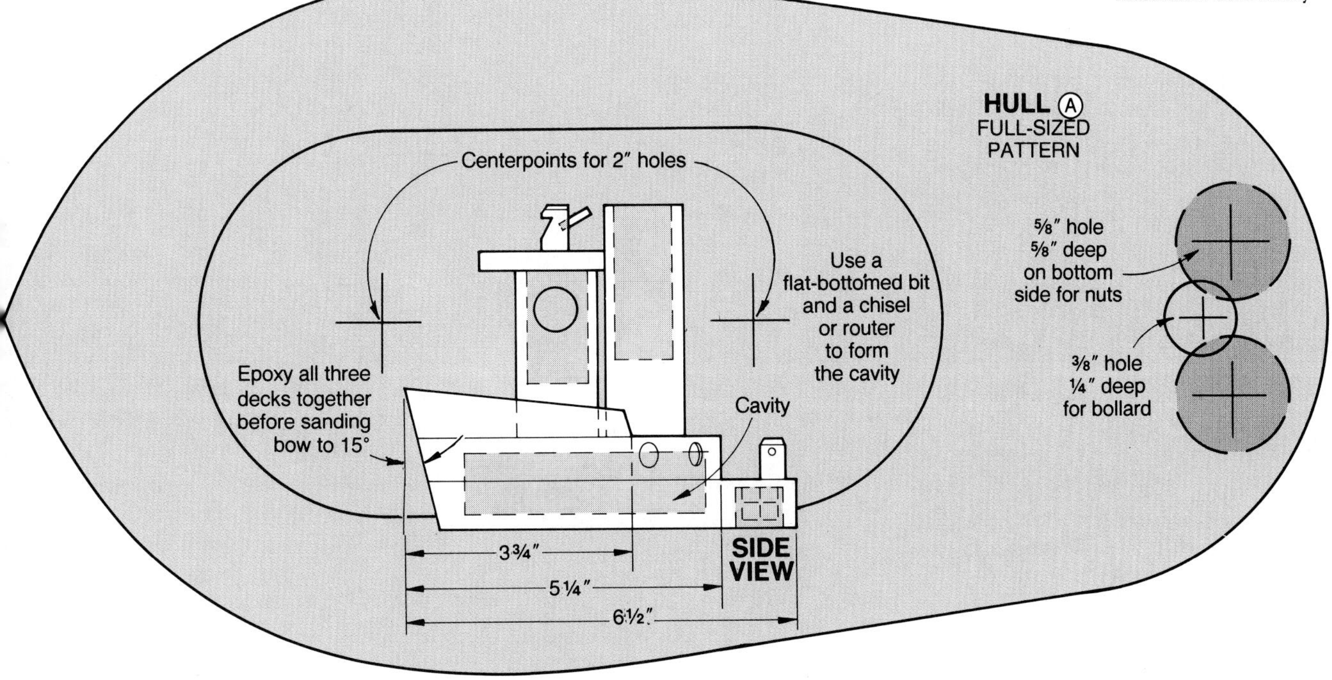

HULL A
FULL-SIZED PATTERN
Centerpoints for 2″ holes
Use a flat-bottomed bit and a chisel or router to form the cavity
Cavity
Epoxy all three decks together before sanding bow to 15°
5/8″ hole 5/8″ deep on bottom side for nuts
3/8″ hole 1/4″ deep for bollard
3 3/4″
5 1/4″
6 1/2″
SIDE VIEW

BARNSTORMING

Steve Bruni, an avid Iowa woodworker and toy designer, modeled this toy after the Curtiss JN-4, a sturdy World War I trainer and observation plane. (You may remember the Jenny from barnstorming shows or as the now-famous plane flying upside down on 100 incorrectly printed airmail stamps.) The toy design proved so popular that Steve and a woodworking buddy, Charles Cullor, constructed and presented nearly 40 Jennies as Christmas gifts for deserving children.

Note: You'll need ¼"-thick stock for this project. You can either resaw or plane thicker stock to size.

The fuselage gets things off the ground

1 Cut two pieces of ¾"-thick stock (we used cherry) to 2¼" wide by 11" long for the fuselage blank (A). Glue and clamp together the pieces face to face with the edges and ends flush. Later, remove the clamps, scrape off the excess glue, and trim the block to 2" wide by 10" long.

2 With a photocopy and spray adhesive, transfer the full-sized fuselage side- and top-view patterns, hole centerpoints, dado and kerf locations, and notch locations to the fuselage blank. (You could also transfer the marks to the blank with carbon paper.)

3 To make a guide for drilling the exhaust ports, cut a piece of scrap 2×4 to 1×1×8" long. Make a mark and miter-cut 2½" from one end where shown on Step 1 of the drawing at *right*. Now, mark diagonals on the square-cut end of the short piece, hold the piece in a handscrew clamp, and use the drill

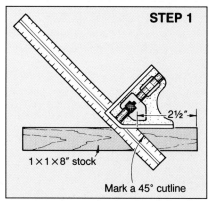

STEP 1

2½"

1 × 1 × 8" stock

Mark a 45° cutline

STEP 2

90°

press and a brad-point bit to drill a ³⁄₁₆" hole centered through it as shown in Step 2 of the drawing.

4 Glue the short piece to the end of the long piece to form the drill guide shown in the photo *below*.

5 Using a combination square, mark a line on the outside face of the drill guide, aligned with the centerpoint of the ³⁄₁₆" hole drilled through the 2½"-long piece.

6 With the outside surface of the guide flush with the top surface of the fuselage blank, align the mark on the side of the drill guide with the marks on the top view, and drill the angled ³⁄₁₆" holes ⅜" deep as shown in the photo on the opposite page. Repeat to drill the holes on the other side of the fuselage.

7 Mark the centerpoint, and drill a ³⁄₁₆" hole ½" deep in the front of the fuselage for the propeller pin (see the Fuselage Patterns Drawing for reference). Switch to a ¼" bit, and drill a pair of holes ⅜" deep into the top surface of the fuselage blank for the wing supports.

BIPLANE

Bill of Materials

Part		Finished Size* T	W	L	Matl.	Qty.
A*	fuselage	1½″	2″	10″	LC	1
B	bottom wing	¼″	2″	11″	C	1
C	top wing	¼″	2½″	11″	C	1
D	strut	¼″	1⅞″	2½″	M	2
E	elevator	¼″	1½″	3⅞″	C	1
F	rudder	¼″	1⅝″	2″	C	1
G	propeller	¼″	⅝″	3¾″	C	1
H	landing gear	¼″	⅝″	2½″	C	2
I	support	¼″	⅝″	2″	C	1
J	headrest	¼″	⅜″	1″	C	1

*Initially cut * part oversized. Trim it to finished size according to the how-to instructions.
Material Key: LC-laminated cherry, C-cherry, M-maple
Supplies: spray adhesive, ⅛″ dowel, ¼″ dowel, 3⁄16″ dowel, two 1¼″-diam. wheels, one ⅞×2⅜″ person, four 3⁄16×¾″ toy axles, finish.

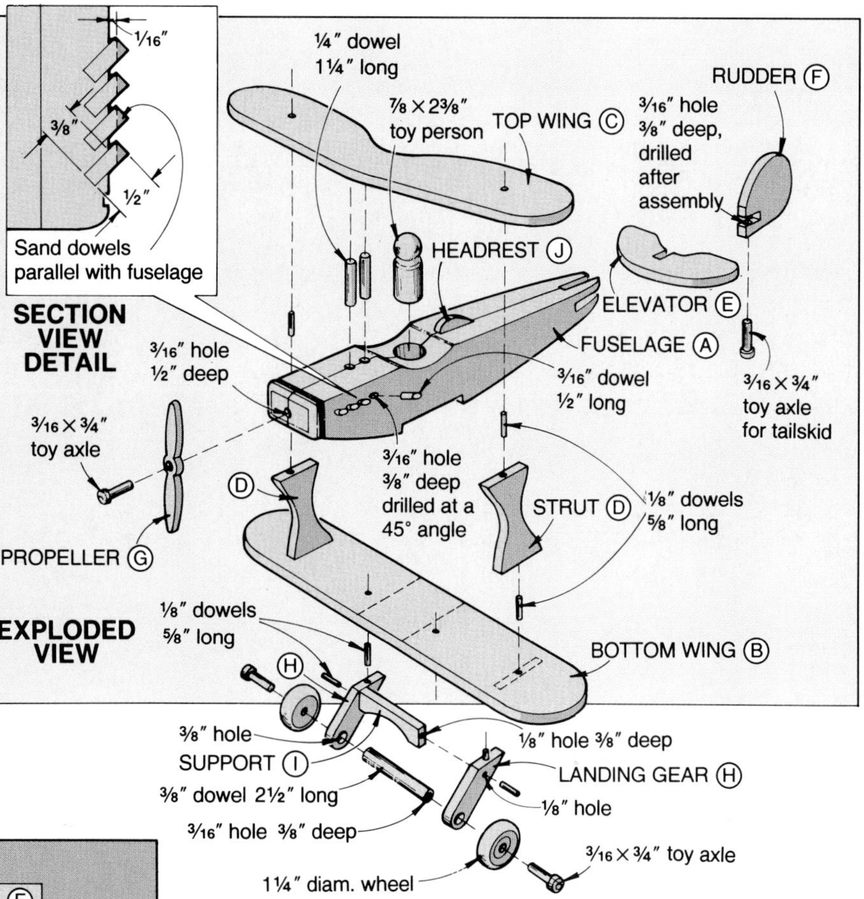

1⁄16″
⅜″
½″
Sand dowels parallel with fuselage
SECTION VIEW DETAIL
¼″ dowel 1¼″ long
⅞×2⅜″ toy person
TOP WING Ⓒ
RUDDER Ⓕ
3⁄16″ hole ⅜″ deep, drilled after assembly
HEADREST Ⓙ
ELEVATOR Ⓔ
FUSELAGE Ⓐ
3⁄16″ hole ½″ deep
3⁄16″ dowel ½″ long
3⁄16×¾″ toy axle for tailskid
3⁄16×¾″ toy axle
3⁄16″ hole ⅜″ deep drilled at a 45° angle
Ⓓ
STRUT Ⓓ
⅛″ dowels ⅝″ long
PROPELLER Ⓖ
⅛″ dowels ⅝″ long
EXPLODED VIEW
BOTTOM WING Ⓑ
Ⓗ
⅜″ hole
SUPPORT Ⓘ
⅜″ dowel 2½″ long
3⁄16″ hole ⅜″ deep
⅛″ hole ⅜″ deep
LANDING GEAR Ⓗ
⅛″ hole
3⁄16×¾″ toy axle
1¼″ diam. wheel

Cutting Diagram

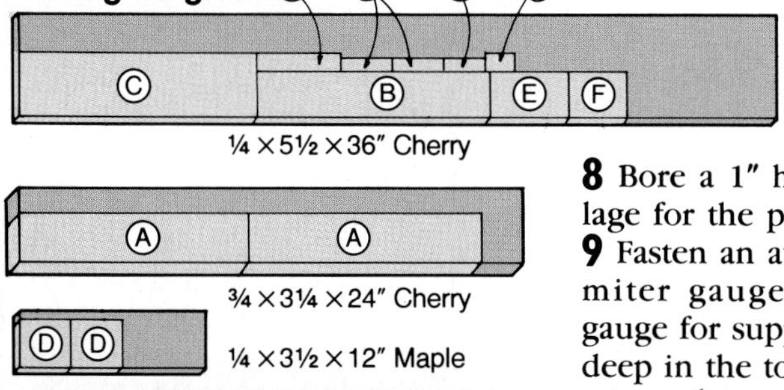

Ⓖ Ⓗ Ⓘ Ⓙ
Ⓒ Ⓑ Ⓔ Ⓕ
¼×5½×36″ Cherry
Ⓐ Ⓐ
¾×3¼×24″ Cherry
Ⓓ Ⓓ
¼×3½×12″ Maple

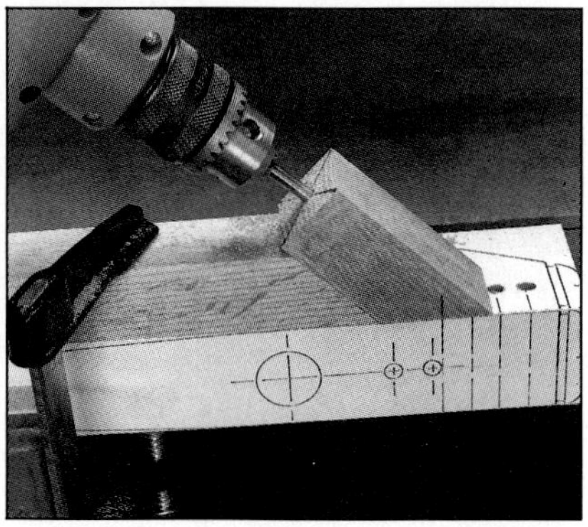

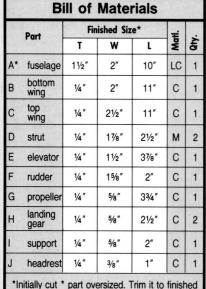

Clamp the drill guide to the fuselage to drill the angled exhaust portholes.

8 Bore a 1″ hole through the fuselage for the pilot.

9 Fasten an auxiliary fence to your miter gauge. Using your miter gauge for support, cut ⅛″ kerfs 1⁄16″ deep in the top and sides of the fuselage. (To keep the kerfs ¼″ from the front of the fuselage, we attached a handscrew clamp to the miter-gauge fence to act as a stop.) Raise your blade 1″ above the saw table and cut the kerf across the bottom edge. See the Fuselage Patterns Drawing for reference.

10 Mount a ¼″ dado blade to your tablesaw and raise the blade to 1″ above the table surface. With the fuselage blank standing on end, use a push block to cut the rudder and elevator notches in the tail as shown in the photo at *right*.

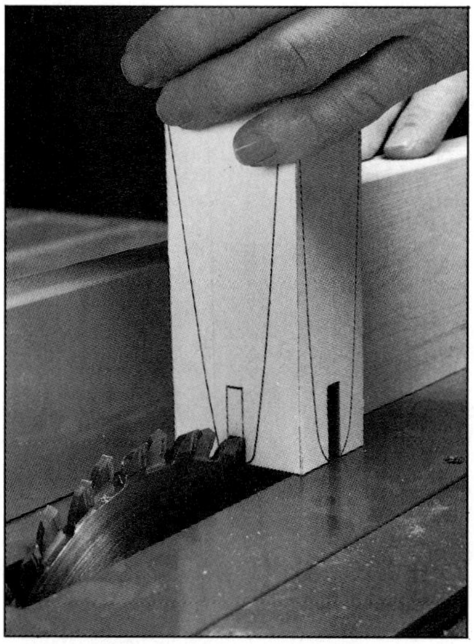

Use a push block when cutting the ¼″ dadoes in the tail section.

Continued

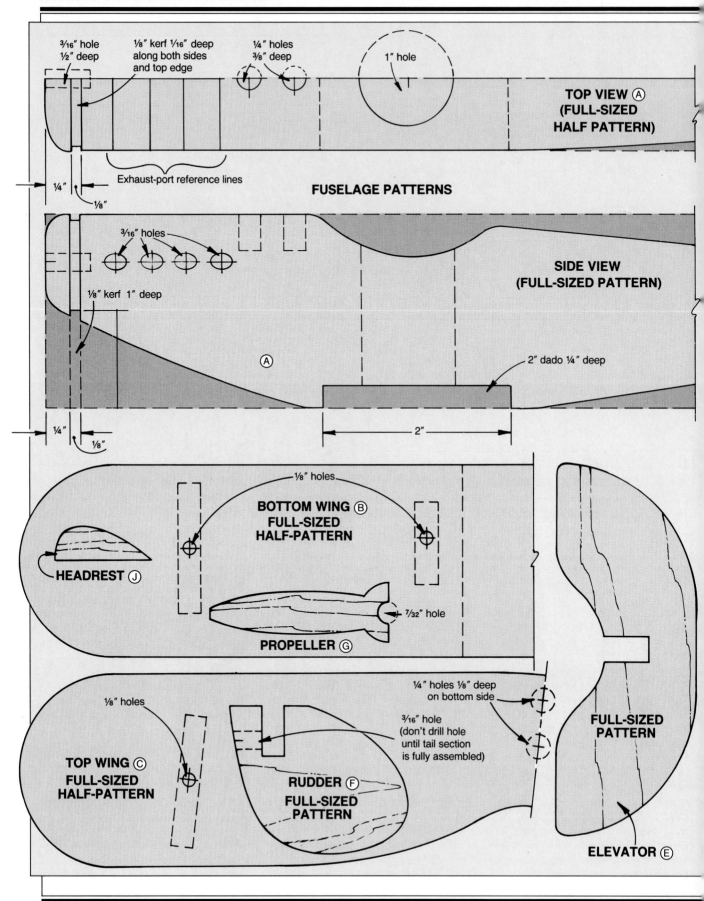

TOP VIEW Ⓐ (FULL-SIZED HALF PATTERN)

3/16" hole 1/2" deep

1/8" kerf 1/16" deep along both sides and top edge

1/4" holes 3/8" deep

1" hole

1/4"

1/8"

Exhaust-port reference lines

FUSELAGE PATTERNS

SIDE VIEW (FULL-SIZED PATTERN)

3/16" holes

1/8" kerf 1" deep

Ⓐ

2" dado 1/4" deep

1/4"

1/8"

2"

1/8" holes

BOTTOM WING Ⓑ FULL-SIZED HALF-PATTERN

HEADREST Ⓙ

7/32" hole

PROPELLER Ⓖ

1/4" holes 1/8" deep on bottom side

3/16" hole (don't drill hole until tail section is fully assembled)

FULL-SIZED PATTERN

1/8" holes

TOP WING Ⓒ FULL-SIZED HALF-PATTERN

RUDDER Ⓕ FULL-SIZED PATTERN

ELEVATOR Ⓔ

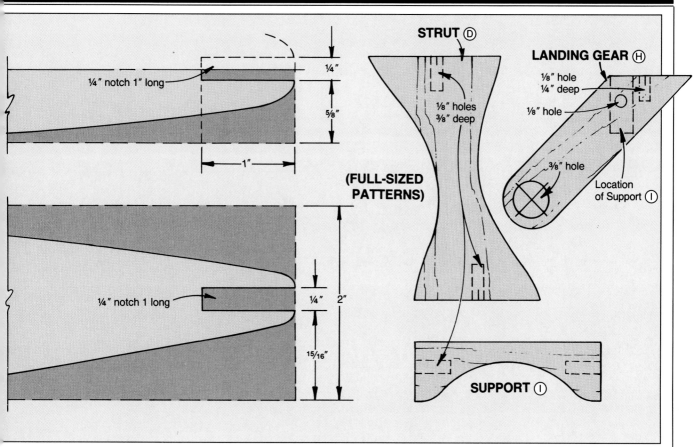

¼" notch 1" long

¼"

5/8"

1"

STRUT Ⓓ

LANDING GEAR Ⓗ

1/8" holes
3/8" deep

(FULL-SIZED PATTERNS)

1/8" hole
¼" deep

1/8" hole

3/8" hole

Location of Support Ⓘ

¼" notch 1 long

¼"
2"

15/16"

SUPPORT Ⓘ

11 Cut a 2"-wide dado ¼" deep across the bottom edge of the fuselage for the bottom wing.

12 With the fuselage on its side, bandsaw the side view to shape. Tape the waste pieces to the fuselage, and cut the top-view pattern to shape. Sand the fuselage smooth.

13 Cut eight 3/16" dowels ½" long, and glue one into each exhaust hole. Sand the ends parallel to the side of the fuselage as shown on the Section View Detail accompanying the Exploded View drawing.

Now, cut and shape the remaining parts

1 Transfer the full-sized patterns and hole centerpoints for the bottom and top wings (B, C), struts (D), elevator (E), rudder (F), propeller (G), landing-gear pieces (H), landing-gear support (I), and headrest (J) to ¼" stock. (We used ¼" cherry for all but the struts; for contrast, we used ¼" maple for those.) Cut the parts to shape. Also, cut a 3/8" dowel 2½" long for the landing-gear axle.

2 Drill the holes where marked, and sand the parts smooth.

The landing gear makes for smooth takeoffs

1 With a brad-point bit in your drill press, drill a 3/16" hole 3/8" deep centered in both ends of the axle.

2 Glue and tape the axle and support (I) between the landing-gear parts (H).

3 Later, drill a pair of 1/8" holes 5/8" deep through the landing gear and into the support. Cut two 1/8" dowels 5/8" long and glue in the holes.

4 With 3/16×¾" toy axles, secure 1¼"-diameter toy wheels to the landing gear. Be careful to keep the wheels spinning freely.

5 With 1/8" dowels, glue and clamp the landing-gear assembly to the underside of the bottom wing (B). If the 1/8" dowels protrude above the top surface of the bottom wing, sand them flush.

Add the wings and propeller

1 Glue and clamp the bottom wing into the dado in the fuselage.

2 Cut four 1/8" dowels 5/8" long. Use two of the dowels to glue and dowel the struts (D) to the bottom wing. Check for square.

3 Cut two ¼" dowels to 1¼" long. Using these two ¼" dowels and the 1/8" dowels cut in the previous step, glue and dowel the top wing (C) to the struts and fuselage.

4 Mount the propeller to the plane with a 3/16×¾" toy axle. To keep the propeller spinning freely, don't push the axle in too far.

Assemble the plane and taxi for takeoff

1 Glue the headrest (J) in place. Glue the elevator (E) and rudder (F) into the tail-section notches.

2 Drill a 3/16" hole 3/8" deep through the elevator. Glue a 3/16×¾" axle peg in the hole to act as a tail skid.

3 Finish-sand the airplane and apply the finish. (We brushed on two coats of polyurethane.) 🍁

Project Design: Steven Bruni
Photographs: Hopkins Associates;
    Jim Kascoutas
Illustrations: Kim Downing; Bill Zaun

Better Homes and Gardens ®

WOOD

FAVORITE TOYS

YOU CAN MAKE

INDEX

Airplanes
  biplane, 92
  Red Baron, 20
Apple Bank, 30
Baja Buggy, 76
Bank, apple, 30
Biplane, 92
Block castle, 86
Boat, 90
Building-block castle, 86
Bulldozer, 53
Carousel, zoo, 45
Cars
  dragster,
  rubber-band-powered, 84
  dune buggy, 76
  four pack, 83
  on tractor/trailer rig, 28
Castle, building block, 86
Chairs
  doll's high chair, 72
  table with, 78
Cradle, doll, 38
Desk, doll, 74
Doll Furniture, 70
  cradle, 38
Dollhouse in a box, 12
Doll stroller, 61
Dragster,
  rubber-band-powered, 84
Duck, waddling, pull toy, 56
Dump truck, 48
Dune buggy, 76
Fat Cat series
  bulldozer, 53
  dump truck and lowboy, 48

Furniture
  doll, 38, 70
  table and chairs, 78
High chair, doll's 72
Horse, rocking, 24
Learning board, 10
Lowboy trailer, 48
Pull toy, waddling duck, 56
Red Baron airplane, 20
Rocking horse, 24
Rubber-band-powered
  dragster, 84
Sleigh, 32
Stroller, doll, 61
Swing, doll 71
Table and Chairs, 78
Tops, turned, 75
Tow Truck, 4
Tractor, 18
Tractor/trailer rigs
  auto transport, 28
  lowboy, 48
Train, 64
Trucks
  hauling cars, 28
  lowboy and
  dump truck, 48
  tow truck, 4
Tugboat, 90
Turnings
  tops, 75
  yo-yo, 44
Yo-yo, turned 44
Zoo carousel, 45